The Art of the

Handwritten

ote

Other Books by Margaret Shepherd

Learn Calligraphy

Using Calligraphy

Capitals for Calligraphy

Borders for Calligraphy

Calligraphy Made Easy

Calligraphy Projects

Calligraphy Alphabets Made Easy

Calligraphy Now (*reissued as* A Manual
of Modern Calligraphy)

Basics of the New Calligraphy

Basics of Left-Handed Calligraphy

Modern Calligraphy Made Easy

Calligraphy for Celebrating Your Wedding

Calligraphy for Celebrating Your Newborn

The Very Small Calligraphy Calendar

The Alphabet Advent Calendar

The ABC Advent Calendar

A Guide

to Reclaiming

Civilized

Communication

BROADWAY BOOKS

NEW YORK

10036

The Art of the

Handwritten

 ote

MARGARET SHEPHERD

Broadway Books titles may be purchased for business or promotional use or for special sales. For information, please write to: Special Markets Department, Random House, Inc., 1540 Broadway, New York, NY 10036.

PRINTED IN THE UNITED STATES OF AMERICA

BROADWAY BOOKS and its logo, a letter B bisected on the diagonal, are trademarks of Broadway Books, a division of Random House, Inc.

Visit our website at www.broadwaybooks.com

Grateful acknowledgment is made to the following:
Gibson Greetings, Inc.: Mother's Day greeting card is reproduced by permission of Gibson Greetings, Inc. © CGI. Note on card is reproduced by permission of the Office of the Honorable William J. Clinton.

The Metropolitan Museum of Art: *La Lettre* by Mary Cassatt. The Metropolitan Museum of Art, Gift of Paul J. Sachs, 1916 (accession # 16.2.9). All rights reserved, The Metropolitan Museum of Art.

Office of Ronald Reagan: President Reagan's letter Nov. 5, 1994, to the American people is reprinted by permission.

Vietnam Memorial photograph by Michael Katakis

Library of Congress Cataloging-in-Publication Data
Shepherd, Margaret.
The art of the handwritten note : a guide to reclaiming civilized communication/Margaret Shepherd.—1st ed.
p. cm.
Includes bibliographical references.
1. Letter writing. 2. Written communication—Social aspects.
3. Letter writing—Social aspects. 4. Penmanship. I. Title.
PE1483 .S425 2002
395.4—dc21   2001035101

Designed by Dana Leigh Treglia

ISBN 0-7679-0745-0

3 5 7 9 10 8 6 4

This book is dedicated to

the memory of my parents,

Geoffrey and Eleanor.

ACKNOWLEDGMENTS

I am grateful to many people for help with this book. I want especially to thank Alison Shepherd Lewis, Winifred Murray Kelley, Janet Murray Fiske, John Deutch, Norma Buxton, Helen Shepherd, June Mamana, Lisbeth Shepherd, Larry LaBlanc, Miriam Friend, Lynn Meservey, Margaret Fitzwilliam, Kirsten Shepherd, Zoe Friend, Lily Friend, Ted Spencer, Bob Boyajian, Heidi Fiske, Peter Davison, Bob Manning, Sebastian Senters Dubrow, Marilyn Brandt, Gareth Dunleavy, Sallie Mitchell at Pilot Pen Company, Megan Kuntze at Crane's, Carole Friedman, Ruth Goldway, Brooke Shearer, Tara McConnell Aukes, Sandy Goroff, Diana Leslie, and many others who listened patiently and contributed generously.

I wish to thank my editor, Tricia Medved, her assistant, James Benson, and my agent, Colleen Mohyde, who kept this book moving along when it seemed to bog down in a mass of details.

I am particularly indebted to my husband, David Friend, for the title and basic idea of this book, and for the encouragement that kept me at it.

CONTENTS

The Handwritten Note Is
Alive and Well

When I mention the handwritten note to any group of otherwise optimistic and intelligent people, I almost always hear someone say, "It's a dying art." Wrong! It's not dying, it's healthier than ever. But it certainly is an art, because it brings out the best in both the person who creates it and the person who looks at it.

The handwritten note has so many virtues that you ought to reach for pen and paper first, before you pick up the phone or move the mouse. In contrast to a phone call, a handwritten note doesn't arrive demanding to be read when you've just sat down to dinner; it courteously lets you know who sent it even before you open it; you won't be annoyed by the sounds coming from the pens of compulsive note-writers at the next table in your favorite restaurant. You'll never get a busy signal from a mailbox; you won't have to play "note tag" to get read; and your readers won't use "note waiting" to put you on hold while they open a note that arrives while they're opening yours. And in contrast to e-mail, a handwritten note looks beautiful and feels personal; you won't get an electronic virus from opening a handwritten note nor find a list of last week's lamebrained jokes. You can still write a note by candlelight when your electricity fails, and mail your note while your server is down.

The handwritten note has been around for hundreds of years, and it's not going to die out just because some of its everyday functions have been taken over by e-mail and voice mail. Adapting to the needs of every fresh generation, it continues to connect people. In fact, a handwritten note is even more vital now than it was a few years ago because it's less routinely used. A note in the mail brightens a dreary landscape of junk mail, form letters, and prefabricated greeting cards, and it shines through a virtual blizzard of abrupt digital memos and disembodied voice chat. When a handwritten note comes in the mail, people pay special attention to what it says. It announces beyond a doubt that the reader really matters to you. Your handwriting insures that your words will be read and thought about in a way that can't be mimicked by print, e-mail, or voice. Handwritten notes are not going to die out, because people still love to receive them and they value each note more as they receive fewer of them.

But the handwritten note has an intrinsic value beyond its rarity. It's not just an antiquarian curiosity, it's an extremely useful tool. It upgrades a wide variety of messages, transforming "Oops" into "Please accept my apology," and "Got the money" into "Thank you for your generosity." Ink on paper is still the classiest way to express the thoughts that really matter, on the occasions that really count. And sometimes it's the only way; your words will carry sympathy and gratitude with a special kind of sincerity when your reader sees them on paper in your writing.

Furthermore, the handwritten note does more than inspire the reader who reads it; it inspires the writer who writes it. Your words not only look better when you write them, but the act of writing them enables you to choose better words. You'll probably be pleasantly and mysteriously surprised to find that the flowing line of pen and ink lets you express yourself in ways that key tapping just doesn't allow.

Corresponding on paper lets you elevate a simple pleasure into an art form. And art has always survived technology. A handwritten note is like dining by candlelight instead of flicking on the lights, like making a gift instead of ordering a product, like taking a walk instead of driving. Handwritten notes will add a lot to your life. You can still use the telephone or the Web for the daily chores of staying in touch, but for the words that matter, it's courteous, classy, caring, and civilized to pick up a pen.

Dear Reader,

Thank you for choosing this book. It will help you write notes that you enjoy writing and people enjoy reading.

Don't worry if you're out of practice or your handwriting doesn't feel perfect. I flunked "script" in Third Grade but still went on to master the pen. If I can do it, anybody can.

I'm sure you will have fun learning this art. Once you get started, you will find yourself writing the kind of notes that keep you connected in the very best way. Stay in touch.

Sincerely,
Margaret

The Art of the

Handwritten

ote

I

Good Reasons to Stop Making Excuses

Writing by hand makes you look good on paper and feel good inside. Even an ordinary handwritten note is better than the best e-mail, and a good handwritten note on the right occasion is a work of art. It says to the reader, "You matter to me, I thought of you, I took trouble on your behalf, here's who I am, I've been thinking of you in the days since this was mailed, I want to share with you the textures and colors and images that I like." And that's just the *unspoken* messages, the pleasure anticipated before the reader even reads the words that the pen and paper have inspired you to choose. The reader can reread what you sent and save it and think good thoughts about you. A note can deliver all this for less than a dollar's worth of materials and ten minutes of your time.

Now ask yourself, do you write enough of these notes? Do you write *any*? If not, why not? There's no excuse not to write a handwritten note; but many people who love to receive notes still let themselves get bogged down with excuses not to send them. Perhaps you'll recognize yourself in one of the ten major whines below; if you do, you can use the suggestions to inspire you to solve what's holding you back from writing the notes you'd like to send.

Take a minute to tell yourself, honestly and in complete sentences, what keeps you from writing. Now read on, to see if your reasons turn out to sound just like everyone else's excuses.

1. "I'm too busy." It's not just the five minutes it takes to write, address, and stamp the note—the average telephone call takes longer than that, even without all the phone tag. You probably make time to do other nonessential activities like cooking for guests, sports, woodworking, watching television, instant messaging, Net surfing, needlework, reading, playing cards, decorative table-settings, social dancing, and gift wrapping. Anyone can find an hour once a week to write. You could write a couple of notes every day if you used the hours you stare at your computer screen and the minutes you spend on hold. Plan ahead to make time to write.

2. "Nobody writes notes anymore." People may not be writing *as many* routine notes as before, but for any special occasion a note is still the very best way to communicate. New technology doesn't always push out the old. People still draw when they could photograph, go to a play although a movie is available, go to movies when they could stay home and watch television, knit sweaters

when they could buy them, bake cakes when they could purchase them, cook from scratch when they could order in, sing when they could turn on the radio. And they still write by hand. If you think people don't write notes anymore because they're not writing to you, just try writing a few notes to them. When they start to write back, you'll see why a note in the mail is such a special treat.

3. "My handwriting is terrible." Virtually everyone finds fault with their own handwriting, even professional calligraphers like the author of this book. (People often feel the same way when they hear a recording of their own voice.) First, your handwriting is probably not that bad once you've warmed up a bit. You're just out of practice because you don't write a lot every day. Second, your writing probably looks fine to the recipient because they're not as critical of it as you are. Third, people are so pleased to get a handwritten note, they will cut you a lot of slack when it comes to handwriting. They probably like your handwriting because they like you. Fourth, this book offers you a chapter on handwriting improvement techniques that will help you refine, repair, or rescue your script.

4. "I don't have the right kind of stationery." This is easier to fix than handwriting. One simple basic notepaper style will cover almost all your correspondence. And as with handwriting, if you have made a reasonable effort to choose paper that is nice to look at, most people will meet you halfway with a reasonable effort to enjoy what you've written on it.

5. "I don't know what to say." Most people don't know what to say at first. Human beings are not born knowing just what to say on paper. For centuries, people have used books just like this one to get them started with phrases, shortcuts, encouragement, and advice. Go to the pages that give you specific wording to get started on a specific note. Use the words you learned in kindergarten: please, thank you, I'm sorry, good luck, I miss you. The basic things you say out loud will make your point; the effort is appreciated far beyond the exact words you choose. As you write more notes, you will gain confidence that your own voice can speak on paper.

6. "I'm going to see (or telephone or e-mail) them before the note would get there." And believe me, you're going to cringe. Think about all the lame excuses you will be making, compared with how pleasant it will be to hear them start with "Wow! Thanks for that nice note." If you see them immediately after you've mailed the note, you can still glow with the contained happiness that comes from both writing *and* seeing someone, and just tell them to watch their mailbox.

7. "It won't get there in time." Some messages won't wait even for the two to three days some mail can take. A handwritten note may not be the best way to arrange a quick meeting or confirm that a parcel arrived, but it can be surprisingly more efficient than phone tag for a lot of messages. You can e-mail or voice-mail a quick message

that says "note follows" while sending the note too. And some notes can be hand delivered.

8. "I won't have a record of what I wrote." Many people start with a checklist of topics to include, which forms a record of what they wrote. For anything important, especially when you begin to write notes, write or type a rough draft to get the phrasing right and save it. Or photocopy your handwritten note. Or scan it in and e-mail it to your file folder. Or just file it in your brain, the way you remember what you have said out loud to people in conversation.

9. "It's a girl thing." Reaching out to other people is the highest form of human endeavor. Real men write notes, lots of them: for business, in their volunteer work, in their hobbies, in their social life, and within their families. It's the glue that keeps life from fragmenting and lets you show that you care. In recent generations, women may have taken responsibility for staying in touch, but today men can enjoy the experience and rediscover its rewards. (Guys who write notes, like guys who do child care, get extra credit for being savvy enough to know that this is not exclusively women's work.) From Napoleon Bonaparte to George H. W. Bush, the guys in charge have been tireless note-writers. If they could do it, you can too.

10. "I've waited too long and now it's too late." This is the only serious problem on the list, and even then this book can offer you some encouragement. Just do it. Sometimes

a guilty feeling of being a little late can paralyze you; it may not be as late as you fear. *Most people are so pleased to hear from you on paper that they won't hold a serious grudge.* And consider the alternatives—either an awkward apology in person next time you meet them (and you *will*), or an inferior substitute like a phone call or e-mail that are by now just as late as the note, or the awkward stunting or ending of a friendship, where you feel guilty and they feel offended. (If you are late with an obligation to a relative, you can't even end the relationship!) So don't think about not writing a note that's late, and don't make a big fuss in the note about your lateness. Just write the same note now that you should have written then, making a *very brief apology* at the end for being late.

Author's note: If any other excuses are holding you back, the author would be happy to offer you additional help; send, care of the publisher, a handwritten note explaining what prevents you from writing.

Three Ways to Get Started Writing

Once you eliminate the excuses that have kept you from writing, you can start paying attention to the reasons to write. These can be described by the O words *obligations, occasions,* and *opportunities.*

OBLIGATIONS: NOTES THAT YOU OWE

When someone dies, when you have hurt someone, or when you have been given a gift, a handwritten note is the *only way* to communicate your feelings of sympathy, apology, or gratitude. You don't have to do more than send your words on paper, but you must not do less. You deserve that black cloud over your head when you don't write, because your silence has made someone think you don't care. You deserve that shining halo over your head when you do write, because that note is going to show your reader that you do care. When a note you owe is written, stamped, and mailed, you will rightly feel that you are in a state of grace.

OCCASIONS: NOTES THAT KEEP RELATIONSHIPS ON TRACK

There are many other times when a handwritten note is the *best way* to be in touch. You can use notes to celebrate a birthday, a holiday, or an achievement; to congratulate on a minor triumph; or to commiserate on a setback. Once you start to send notes on special occasions, you will discover ordinary occasions that can be elevated into special occasions with a note. Although you can always reach for the phone or e-mail, or buy a greeting card, the note means so much more. And the habit of sending notes on occasions will make it easier for you to be ready to send the ones you owe.

OPPORTUNITIES: NOTES THAT OPEN
NEW WAYS TO CONNECT

The handwritten note opens up an *extra way* to stay in touch, when you might not have thought of sending or saying anything. If you begin to use handwritten notes routinely, you can then start to use them creatively when inspiration strikes. A handwritten note opens new channels of communication when you write to a small child, stay in touch with the elderly, thank people for kindness, add your own words to gifts, and comment on clippings. A note gives you the opportunity to stay connected with people you care about in ways you might not have thought about.

"The fondness for writing

grows with writing."

—EPICIETUS, 100 A.D.

II

Getting in Touch with Yourself

and with Each Other

People used to write mail conversationally, receiving a letter and then answering it in return. Sometimes the letter got there the same day; sometimes it took months. Today, much of that back-and-forth on paper has been taken over by telephone conversations, printed greetings, e-mail exchanges, and face-to-face encounters. But don't let these convenient shortcuts prevent you from using pen and ink when it would really do a better job.

Your daily regimen of staying in touch probably offers three categories of contact: *verbal* (telephone and meeting), *digital* (e-mail and fax), and *purchased* (gifts and greeting cards). You can learn to use handwritten notes in place of any of these.

Handwrite instead of talk. First, you routinely meet people or talk to them by telephone. Stop and think before you make that phone call or drop by; a note offers you the chance to get your phrasing right, to present exactly the words you want to convey (not more or less), and to catch people at their convenience. You can present your message without all the *um*s, *er*s, and extra small-talk that blurs and dilutes it.

Handwrite instead of type. Second, you routinely e-mail or fax to people. Stop and think about what a handwritten note might add to this flavorless format: Your own handwriting makes your personality come through, the paper you choose has texture and tone, the stamped delivery and private envelope send a clear signal that this is not routine. You might keep a stack of note cards next to your keyboard to remind you to upgrade an occasional onscreen note by simply copying by hand what you've typed and send the note instead of, or in confirmation of, the e-mail. If it doesn't need to be there instantaneously, maybe a note would add a touch of class.

Handwrite instead of buy. Third, on important occasions you routinely send a gift or a greeting card with a prefabricated message. Stop and think about what you'd really like to say to the person in your own words. Then write those words. At the very least (and if you think your reader likes conventional greeting card sentiments) add a salutation and at least two whole sentences before you sign your name.

A note can also replace or accompany a gift. It can be much nicer than something you buy; it is unique, priceless, timeless, and personalized. It can stand out in a crowd of gifts at a wedding or birthday. A note to a bride and groom, for instance, about how special they are to you and how happy you are to see them together will create a memento that lasts long after many gifts are used and used up. A note that comes from the heart is the perfect gift for someone who has everything, and it deepens the meaning of any gift it accompanies.

When you are deciding whether to send a handwritten note in place of your usual communication, remember its advantages and think about how they might work for you:

The handwritten note's rarity heightens its appeal. People give it their attention because they trust that it will repay their attention.

Each handwritten note is unique. Exclusivity is certain; no one else is receiving exactly the same note.

The handwritten note is virus free. People who open a handwritten note can safely assume it comes from someone they know, on a topic they will enjoy. It won't jump out of the envelope, destroy all other letters nearby, or send silly handwritten notes to everyone in their address book.

The handwritten note offers your attention without immediately demanding theirs. They can enjoy the anticipation of opening it when they want to and rereading it at their leisure.

The handwritten note levels the playing field. It facilitates social equality without eliminating courtesy. Virtually everyone can pick up a pen, afford a stamp, and set their thoughts on paper. A person without computer skills can communicate with a whiz kid. A poor person may write to a rich person, a young person to an old person, a subordinate to a boss.

The handwritten note pays debts. If you are under a debt of gratitude to someone or owe them an apology, a handwritten note evens up the social balance.

The handwritten note is private. They can be sure no one else has opened it. Postal regulations insure privacy in the mail.

The handwritten note is self-sufficient but also gregarious. Your note is complete in itself, but you can choose to enclose something else in the envelope with it.

The handwritten note endures, but can also be destroyed. A note can be saved for centuries or be put into the fire immediately. A good note can be shared with others; a real stinker can be sent back to the writer.

With all these virtues, the handwritten note has only a few disadvantages. Perhaps the main drawback is external: Mail delivery takes an *unpredictable number of days;* the very best you can hope for is the once-a-day mail delivery sometime tomorrow. If it goes astray, you may not know for weeks. You cannot know exactly when it will arrive, or prove that it has arrived, unless you pay for certified or registered mail, a mechanism that detracts from its personal quality. You must have stamps to put on it and you must know how much postage it requires. You may have to go to a mailbox or post office to send it. But the handwritten note is still the best way to participate in the inspiring cycle of sending and receiving mail.

How to Send the Note You Wrote

Even before you start writing a note, you can choose from a number of ways to send it. The arrival of your note can deliver all kinds of unspoken messages about how much effort you spent, how friendly you feel toward the person, what your relative social status is, how well acquainted the two of you are, how private your relationship is, how formal you would like to be, and what your values are in human relations.

The usual way to send a note, of course, is to stick a stamp on it and mail it. But if the receiver lives nearby, you can hand-carry it, delivering it personally or to the doorstep or mailbox. You can have a parcel delivery service or bicycle messenger carry it, or include it in a flower delivery.

If the note is going even closer, to someone under the same roof (at home, at school, or at work), there are a number of creative ways to send it. You can hand it to them or to a go-between, set it on their desk, tape it to their door, prop it on a pillow, tack it to a message board, put it in a pigeonhole, enclose it with a gift, or include in their lunch box. Figure out where they are most likely to look and position it there—on their mirror, doorknob, refrigerator, or laptop.

"Fine writing is next to fine doing"

—JOHN KEATS

The Arrival of a Handwritten Note

Part of the pleasure of sending a handwritten note is picturing its arrival.

Visualize the person sorting through the flotsam and jetsam of junk mail, grocery store specials, institutional fund-raising, event announcements, and bills—a dreary landscape of low-interest clutter that is suddenly brightened by a treasure. It's like a gift; *the anticipation that leads up to opening a handwritten note adds to the actual pleasure for both the giver and the receiver.*

The envelope has a *functional job* to do—to get the enclosed letter safely to the reader. The name must be clear and the information in the address must be accurate. These words and numbers must be arranged in a prescribed design so that the machine or person who sorts the mail doesn't have to guess at what is written.

But the envelope also has a *ceremonial job* to do: to prepare the reader to enjoy reading what is in the note. Some of your readers will enjoy recognizing you by your handwriting, noticing the color match between ink, stamp, liner, and paper, and picking up on the decorative touches that express who you are. Other times you may need to keep the extra decoration to a minimum. But always give your note the dignity it deserves by putting it in an envelope.

The envelope is a crucial element in how the note is perceived. When impersonal mail arrives, you know what is inside it just by glancing at the envelope; the contents of mass mail are al-

most always as impersonal as the envelope and you rarely get a pleasant surprise. Most days, your mail reaffirms several dreary suspicions—that you are only a name on a list, that someone wants something from you but didn't think it was worth spending much effort asking you, that the world is as indifferent as you suspected. In contrast, if you receive a note, you can enjoy the ritual of opening it with the sure knowledge that although you cannot know exactly what it will say and how it will look, you can already guess at who wrote it and know that it is one of a kind, that it is meant only for you, and that you are worth the effort it took. Inside that envelope is evidence that someone wants to be in touch with you for some very good reason. And that's one of the greatest human experiences; receiving the gift of another person's attention.

The recipient sits down to read your note already anticipating that they will hear in their head the voice of someone they know, probably saying something they will enjoy. For a few minutes you will seem to be there with them through the power of the hand-written word. In the next chapter we look at ways to be sure that when your reader receives a note from you, it speaks—on paper—clearly with your voice.

"*Life is not so short but that*

there is always time

enough for courtesy."

—RALPH WALDO EMERSON

III

How to Express Who You Are on Paper

When you write a note, you are giving yourself to the reader in the most civilized way. A handwritten note is a unique gesture that offers more of you without demanding more of them. Writing shows the mark of your own hand and your choices of real materials, and mailing shows that the message comes from a person in a real place. You cannot get the same effect even if you simply transmit the image of your handwriting, as logic might suggest, because the paper and ink itself tell about you. And the envelope frames the whole work of art with the added pleasure of anticipation.

Art is about choices. A work of art is made up of what the artist has decided is important. Your note is your opportunity to create art by making choices. Choosing to write by hand in the first place is a magnificent choice that means you care about connecting with people. The next choices you make show how committed you are to using the best *materials, handwriting,* and *wording.*

A handwritten note has at least three dimensions; it is a crafted object made of materials, it is a work of art that can be enjoyed visually, and it is literature composed of words. When your note arrives, it speaks to the reader in these three important ways. You have chosen paper and pen that you like; your handwriting is as good as you can make it; and your words say what you mean. Here is how you can make sure that these choices carry out your intentions.

Materials: Your Paper

Writing paper gives the reader all kinds of nonverbal messages. The stationery you choose from comes in different page sizes. The paper can be thick or thin, stiff or soft, speckled or pure, rough or smooth, printed or plain, deckle-edged or clean-cut, tinted or white. You can buy stationery already printed with a decorated border, an initial, or a raised pattern, or have plain paper custom-printed with your address, name, initials, or insignia. To decide what style of stationery to buy, think about who you are: Do you like to speak softly or make a splash, do you dress in tailored formality or casual comfort, are you enterprising or cautious? Will you be mostly writing to people your age and younger, or addressing more traditional older people? Do you want your stationery to meet the conventional expectations of people who may not know you well, or can it express your individuality to close friends and family?

Start by browsing the stationery section of your nearest department store, card shop, or gift store. Paper for good stationery is made with more cotton and linen fiber than ordinary paper, which is usually all wood fiber. In addition, writing paper is coated with a smooth gel called size or sizing that keeps the paper from blotting up the ink like a paper towel. Read the labels and ask for advice. If you have received a note you like from someone whose taste you admire, bring in the note and ask for something like it.

Choose your paper in person, using all your senses; feel the surface and weight and stiffness of any paper before you buy it, inhale its aroma, and write with your favorite pen on what you have bought before you buy much more of it.

Guidelines on a separate sheet will show through lightweight paper (twenty pound) but unfortunately much of the nicest paper is heavy enough to keep you from seeing guidelines through it. The slightly lined appearance of some paper, however, can help you level out your horizontally challenged writing; ask for "laid" paper, which looks faintly ridged, like corduroy; "wove" paper is the same flat texture all over, like felt. Recycled paper has small flecks or fibers in it. "Parchment" paper has an artificially uneven

When in doubt, choose simple notepaper. You can always pep up plain stationery with stickers, stamps, attachments, and drawings, but it's hard to tone down something that is already imprinted. A puppy printed on the corner of a condolence note is appropriate only if you are under twelve.

tone to evoke aged medieval manuscript parchment. Watch out for too much background tone, which distracts both writer and reader.

Consider how much you want to spend. Good stationery is expensive, partly because it is made of good fiber and handled with extra care to make the surface friendly to the pen, but also because it carries subtle information about your taste (or not so subtle, as when an expensive store's name is embossed on the envelopes, the printing is intricate, or the lining of the envelopes is clearly out of the ordinary). Spend as much as you can comfortably afford. It is better to spend too much than too little. All but the most costly notes come in a range of styles, and the boost that good paper gives to your morale can do a lot to improve your script and wording, and help motivate you to write in the first place.

Beautiful materials do inspire you to write better. But top-quality stationery may not be right for you if the cost of each note makes you reluctant to write or afraid of making a mistake. Start writing with medium-priced notepaper; don't waste your effort with cheap paper. If the price still worries you, write a rough draft on scratch paper to ensure that mistakes don't waste whole note cards. As a rule of thumb, a high-quality note card and its envelope should still cost about half the price of an ordinary greeting card.

Think about stationery size. If you are accustomed to the condensed wording of e-mail, maybe you will continue to express yourself best on one side or two sides of a stiff note card. If you like to leave generous margins, add news, go into detail, and use long words, a larger note on flexible paper that folds double to a little less than the size of the note card will allow your thoughts to expand. And if you like to fill up whole pages with long, leisurely letters, then be sure you have sheets of personal-size (5″ by 7″) or even business-size (8½″ by 11″) letter stationery. Furthermore, the size of your pen and your handwriting will govern how much paper you need to allow. If you need to write notes for a very formal occasion, where etiquette is going to matter, get advice about the proper size that people may expect in this context.

Sometimes a little economy can drain a lot of warmth out of your note: A foldover self-mailer may seem like a nicely informal version of a personal note, but it is a big step down in terms of how it feels, subconsciously, to the reader. If the message expresses thanks or sympathy, they may feel subtly slighted without being able to say why. To put your words in the best light, buy notecards *with envelopes* and use them.

You can buy note cards already printed with your first or last initial. If you want to special-order monogrammed stationery, you can follow the European custom of enlarging your last initial and adding your first initial at the left and your middle at the right. If you use only two names, pair your two initials. Or experiment with other combinations.

Be wary of ordering personal stationery from a business printer. Even if you like the way the samples feel and look, you may be disappointed when you write on them. Most of these business stationery papers are designed to accept printer or copier ink and may not provide the best surface for ink from a pen, especially a fountain pen.

Starting out: A dozen cream-colored note cards or folded notes are the best all-purpose style to start with if you can choose only one. You can't go wrong with simplicity. A box of notes, twelve stamps, and an inexpensive fountain pen will cost you less than two tickets to the movies. As soon as you have used up your first box of notes, reward yourself with something special, like a raised-monogram or a high-quality printed image.

Materials: Your Pen

The pen you choose to write with will shape your thoughts as much as it shapes your script. Your pen should make you feel confident about your ability to write your words the way you would like them to be read.

For most people who discover or rediscover the art of the handwritten note, the fountain pen makes the highest-quality visual image with moderate expense and minimal struggle. The ink is dense, the width of the line varies expressively, the pen strokes glide over the paper, you feel more inspired.

You can also write well with dozens of everyday markers and ballpoints, which are widely available and easy to use.

Fountain pens, markers, and old-fashioned dip pens also offer the option of a calligraphy nib for italic writing.

A fountain pen writes through capillary action that pulls the ink out of the reservoir, down under the metal nib, and out onto the paper through the thin slit in the point. The ink is just thin enough to flow smoothly but thick enough to make a sharp, dramatic line, and the point of most fountain pens gives the line a slight variation that makes it interesting to look at but easy to read.

Dry weather sometimes stops the flow. A damp tissue can clear away any dried ink and a little water can start the flow.

The opposite problem, too much ink flow, may occur for three simple reasons: falling barometric pressure or cabin pressure, air pressure from within a nearly empty cartridge, extra ink remaining on the nib from recent refilling. The leak is caused not by the ink but by the air in the reservoir that expands when the pressure outside the pen drops. To prevent the ink from leaking out, keep the pen filled and store it pointing up with the cap on. Use the ink that is recommended for the pen. (Some inks have different viscosity for different nib tolerances.) And don't write with a partly filled pen in an airplane; when the pressure in the cabin changes, your pen may leak.

Most fountain pens use transparent water-based inks. In damp weather you may need to let a page of handwriting dry for a few seconds; some lefthanders may find that their pen hand needs slight repositioning to avoid smearing the fresh ink. In ages past, people dusted their pages with special fine sand to dry the ink, or carefully rocked a curved blotter across it.

While the more expensive fountain pens have points made of

gold or iridium, you can start with an inexpensive fountain pen to see if you want to save up for a fancy one. Best high-end brands: Mont Blanc, Pelikan, Waterman, Rotring. Widely available mid-price brands: Parker, Shaeffer, Estabrook, Sanford, Cross, Osmiroid. Best value: Pilot Varsity, a disposable fountain pen.

A *marker* is made of a bundle of stiff fibers that mops a thin, unvarying track of ink onto the page. The ink is thinner than fountain pen ink. Various ink formulas balance the need for the ink to stay wet in the pen with the need for it to be dry on the page. Marker ink is a dye, so some colors will fade in the light and smear if moistened; some of the more permanent inks can soak through the paper to show on the back. After a while the point of a marker wears out or dries up, and the ink eventually gets used up too. When the pen is used up, you can just spend a dollar or two to buy a new marker in a brand that you like.

A *ballpoint* has the advantage of writing virtually everywhere. A rolling ball in the point lays down a track of thick oil-based waterproof ink that sticks to many kinds of surfaces, including some kinds of paper that would blot or repel a fountain pen. A rollerball is similar but writes with thinner ink that flows more readily. (You can visualize what's going on inside these pens by comparing ballpoint ink to toothpaste and rollerball ink to shampoo.) Most ballpoint brands sold in office stores, drugstores, and stationery stores are similar in their quality of line. Souvenir pens bought in quantity are often just too cheap to write well.

The most important thing about your pen is how it feels to you as its point travels over the surface of the paper. Your pen should get the ink onto the paper without a struggle.

A pen can be a beautiful object that looks like a piece of jewelry in your pocket and feels like a magic wand in your hand. But the most beautiful pen won't do you any good if it doesn't help you write. If you have trouble with it, don't give up on the pen or on the project of handwriting your notes. A pen is just a tool: You can master it to work for you. Study the pluses and minuses that each pen offers and be sure you don't overreact to minor problems at first.

The costliest new pens go to connoisseurs who buy them to look at, not write with. Most of these limited editions are offered in jewelry stores and specialized pen stores as ballpoints or roller balls; they contain the same standardized refills that go into cheaper pens, so that if you spend more than about twenty dollars, the extra money won't have any effect on the kind of line the pen makes on the page.

Though a ballpoint is not an inspiring pen to write with, you can try *four simple ways* to make your ballpoint nicer to handle and easier to read. Store it pointing up so a blob of ink doesn't collect at the point. Pad your writing surface with several sheets of plain paper to give the point some extra traction on the surface so it doesn't skid around. Buy medium rather than fine widths. If the pen won't write, hold it near a flame for two seconds to get the ink to flow smoothly again.

FIND YOURSELF CHOOSING A PEN

Choose a pen that expresses how you feel about who you are. See if any of these writers sound like you, either the way you are or the way you'd like to appear.

If you enjoy historical authenticity,
write with a dip pen and india ink.

If you're direct and practical, write
with a thin-line marker or rollerball.

To express your individuality,
write with a calligraphy pen.

IF script is a simple tool for communication, use a medium ball-point.

If you've been the same person since
7th grade, use a blue cartridge pen.

IF you like to surprise people, write
with sparkles or silver on black.

If you take pleasure in fine possessions,
treat yourself to a classic fountain
pen and engraved stationery.

You can be a medieval monk
with feather quill & parchment...

...a Chinese scholar with a brush...

...a Venetian correspondant with a glass pen...

...or a Victorian antiquarian with a metal dip pen.

THE OTHER END OF THE PEN

Although the most important part of the pen is the point, your writing is also influenced by how the whole pen feels in your hand and appeals to your eye. Each person will find the right combination of the pen's weight, its length, its thickness, its shape, its surface texture. If beautiful materials inspire you to make the beautiful letters that will then help you shape beautiful phrases, you should treat yourself to a collector's fountain pen. But no matter how much you spend, you can't just assume that precious materials in the handle of the pen will automatically guarantee valuable writing on the page.

If you want to own a fine pen or give one as a gift, here are some suggestions about choosing, using, and preserving it:

> You should spend some time trying out pens before you buy. Talk to your friends about what they use, but don't be surprised if the truly serious pen owners don't want to lend you their pens to try out. (See next point.)

> The metal point of a fountain pen wears down a little, through friction and pressure, to suit your own writing angle and direction; if anyone else writes with it, they may change the feel.

> A cheap fountain pen is still usually better than an expensive ballpoint. Spend your money on the nib before splurging on the pen body; what happens at the point is more important than how the pen looks.

≈ Beyond about twenty dollars, an expensive ballpoint does not write much better than a cheap ballpoint.

≈ Use the pen whenever you can. It gets better with use, and you get accustomed to it. Take it with you everywhere. Draw with it, doodle with it, and sign your name a hundred times with it.

≈ Write at various letter sizes until you find the best one for your pen and your hand, then stick to it.

≈ Try not to jab the fountain pen nib into soft or damp paper that may snag the tip and twist it.

≈ If you are choosing a calligraphy pen, remember that a wide marker is better for lettering practice and a narrow fountain pen is better for handwriting notes.

≈ Always recap the pen and store it with the nib pointing up.

≈ Use only fountain pen ink or cartridges; thicker india ink will clog it and corrode it.

Whatever pen you choose, embrace it. If you always write with this pen, you strengthen your identity on paper for your reader. It will give your handwriting more confidence and consistency, developing into a "signature style." With the right pen, your handwriting will begin to look like the real you—to your reader and to yourself.

Handwriting

Your handwriting reveals you in a number of ways. The fact that you choose to write by hand at all shows that you are not afraid to give something of yourself to other people, and that you think some civilized forms of communication are worth extra effort. The pen you have chosen immediately gives your writing a look that makes it uniquely yours. And your fingers, no matter how you reeducate them, still are guided by signals from the same old brain you've always used.

You may be motivated to try to *improve your handwriting*. Decide how much improvement you want, and then read the suggestions about how you can make it happen and maintain it. REFINE: Upgrade from basic to calligraphic REPAIR: Upgrade from poor to good. RESCUE: Upgrade from awful to passable.

REFINE YOUR HANDWRITING.

Daily practice with any pen ensures some improvement, and the right calligraphy pen will immediately make a dramatic difference. You can transform your script into italic calligraphy if you are motivated to do ten minutes of practice every day for a month. Practice on lined paper, and when you write notes, choose stationery that lets a guideline sheet show through (or use a light table). If you want more calligraphy instruction, you can go even further into italic and other lettering styles with my *Learn Calligraphy: The Complete Book of Lettering and Design*.

Refine your handwriting with daily practice in the basics of Italic calligraphy. Repeat each exercise at least twice on separate lines.

Warm up before practice
1. Zigzag

2. Drape

3. Arch

4. Circle and Bar

5. Spacing should be even

Try wider or closer spacing to find your personal style

6. Slant all the letters about 5 degrees

7. Extenders go almost to the next line

Practice similar letter shapes together

8. Drape: *u y g d q a*

u u u

9. Arch: *n h b p r m*

n n n

10. Connect some letters

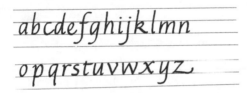

unop   vation

11. Practice each letter alone, in groups, and in words

abcdefghijklmn

opqrstuvwxyz

Try· *The quick brown fox jumps over the lazy dog.*

12. Numerals

1 2 3 4 5 6 7 8 9 0

To improve how your script looks and make it more readable without trying to change your habits, just start your notewriting sessions with these warm-up exercises.

≈ Breathe evenly. Sit comfortably. Hold the pen loosely. Warm up with up-and-down strokes that extend from one to three lines tall.

≈ Don't try to change the way you shape most of your letters or how you usually connect them, but do fix up a few specific single letters: The ubiquitous M in Mr. and Ms. and (a dozen) states; D of Dear; S of Street and Sincerely; Y of yours and yes; and T that starts The, This, To, and That. You'll also enjoy fixing up your own signature and your own initials by repeating them—try twenty-five times—until you create some improvement.

≋ Lay a guideline sheet under your notepaper—even if the lines don't show up clearly, they will establish reference points to give you a target at both sides (see page 156).

RESCUE YOUR HANDWRITING

It may be beyond your ambition to redesign your writing. But don't write off the handwritten note just because you're not proud of your script; there are still half a dozen simple ways to make your handwriting good enough to put your ideas across without a struggle for you or your reader. These six quick fixes can upgrade anyone's script.

≋ First, use a pen you really like, a fountain pen if possible. Most writing looks much better right away with the fountain pen's intense ink, definite line, and slight variation in width; and then because you get positive visual feedback, you begin to relax and actually shape the letters better.

≋ Second, write on paper that looks and feels good but not paper that is so precious it makes you worry about using it up.

∾ Third, get comfortable in your chair, cheer up about your life, sweeten your other senses.

∾ Fourth, don't just warm up with loops and coils; psych yourself up by writing a few lines of positive phrases on scratch paper.

∾ Fifth, get all the mistakes out of your system in a rough draft. Handwriting is more of a pleasure when some of the work of composing the words is already done.

∾ Finally, *have fun* with writing: Play with swashes, look around you at letters that you like, write jokes, poems, quotations. Writing doesn't have to be a chore. It's yours to enjoy and share, no matter how inexpert you may think it looks.

To some extent, how you write is who you are. In the same way that you cannot choose your body but you can exercise and stand up straight, you cannot alter your handwriting much but you can exercise it and correct its posture. Writing does convey an impression of the person who writes it, but that impression is under your control.

Your writing reveals you the way your face reveals you: The fact that you are smiling is more important than the fact that you are beautiful. Despite what many graphologists claim, your handwriting does not reveal secrets about your personality. But you can assess your personality type and try to strengthen those aspects of your writing that you think will portray you most clearly.

Accept yourself when you write; if you judge your own handwriting too harshly, your hand and body will tense up. Be as tolerant of your own script as you are of others'. In a recent national survey conducted by Pilot Pen Company, only a third of respondents rated their own handwriting above average ("good"), while two-thirds of them said a person's handwriting did not influence their opinion of that person.

Your handwriting also changes depending on mood, materials, purpose, text, distractions, and something as simple as the height of your chair. You may be feeling leisurely or rushed, shy or exuberant, upbeat or downcast. Your handwriting can let those feelings come through if you want it to (and even sometimes if you don't want it to). If you would like to control the effect that mood has on your handwriting, try looking in the mirror and making the facial expression that symbolizes how you feel or would like to feel. (A mirror will also help you make better telephone calls.) Then write a few phrases about your state of mind. *I'm looking at a peaceful landscape. I couldn't wait to tell you. I've been wondering. Remember me? Guess what?! I've met the most wonderful guy. I miss you terribly. Congratulations. I'm afraid we don't have a lot in common. I'm so sorry.*

Wording

After you have defined yourself through your pen and paper and the handwriting you create with them, your wording adds the third dimension, one that may be the simplest element to create. For many of the notes you send, there are limits already implicit in the occasion that guide you to the right things to say. Once you know a few phrases to use or avoid, you can get started with your own phrases.

Choosing words is like choosing clothes. You can learn to express who you are within the limits of what is expected of you. Naturally, you know that you should dress formally for a funeral, festively for a wedding, informally for a cookout; you similarly tailor and accessorize your note to the tone of the occasion. Through practice in writing notes, and through attention to the notes you receive, you will develop a sense of what's expected and what's allowed in different situations.

You can convey many shadings of tone with the materials, writing, and wording of even the simplest note. For instance, there are dozens of ways people can choose to greet each other when they meet in person. How you say hello depends on who you are and where you are and how old you are and whom you are greeting and when you last saw each other and what has happened since then. You choose without even thinking from these possible spoken greetings: How do you do, good morning, hello, hi, how nice to see you, yo!, hiya, how are you, what's up, 's'up? hola, there you are, ahem. Greeting in person, you can shake hands, give a secret handshake, wave, nod, bow, curtsy, salaam, hug, kiss, kiss the air. You can translate all these personal shades of spoken meaning into the medium of the handwritten note through your choice of pen and paper, handwriting, and the wording of your salutation.

While you can start with the standard phrases and conventional formats shown in this book, and while you should bear in mind whom you are writing to, you should always *be sincere.*

When in doubt, say what you really mean rather than second-guessing what you think the person might be expecting.

> When writing to people who speak a different language from yours, use your own language unless you are very fluent in theirs, as they can always get someone to translate the parts they don't understand; if you make an error in their language, however, they may *never* figure out what you are trying to say.

To have confidence in your own choice of words, before you start to compose a note for a specific purpose you should familiarize yourself with the most obvious dos and don'ts.

Here are the seven deadly sins to avoid and the seven shining virtues to strive for in the materials, handwriting, and wording of any handwritten note:

Don'ts

1. Do not write with a pencil or use blue-lined school paper, especially not notebook paper with holes punched in it. That's like going out dressed only in your underpants. That is only for rough drafts and for people under the age of ten. You can use a ballpoint on plain white paper if you have absolutely no other materials and you need to send a note. That's at least like wearing a T-shirt and jeans.

2. Do not cross out and correct more than two errors per page. That's like going out dressed in clothing that has holes in it. Start over, perhaps with a rough draft first.

3. Notepaper can have "thank you" printed on it but does not need it. The older you get, and the more notes you write, the less you need extra props. You should have confidence that your words, especially the most important ones, will communicate better in your handwriting.

4. Even though your note may be late, do not apologize for your tardiness in the first line. That puts the emphasis on you and sets up a defensive tone.

5. Do not misspell the reader's name. They may forgive you any other misspelling. (Try not to misspell any words at all; when in doubt, look it up, and if you can't find it, call your local library.) A misspelled word in a note is like a belch in a conversation; the reader can pretend not to notice the mistake. A misspelled name is like a slap in the face; they can't pretend not to notice the insult.

6. Do not ever open up anyone else's mail or hold it up to the light. That's stealing. This goes for e-mail and voice mail too, and for private conversations. A securely sealed envelope made of opaque paper or lined with a second layer helps people resist the temptation to peek.

7. Confucius says, "When you are joyful, do not make promises; when you are angry, do not mail a letter." You

are allowed to write that angry letter, but you should always cool down overnight and then destroy it. If you have already mailed the kind of words that can destroy a relationship, call the person and apologize ahead of time for flaming them; ask them to destroy the note or return it unread.

Dos

1. Do include the date, even on a short note. ("Wednesday" is not really enough.) A note is a document that shows what you were thinking at a specific time and place; it can be extremely interesting years later, even to you. A place and a date makes the job of your biographers much easier if you go on to become famous.

2. Do write by hand to express sympathy when someone dies. If you feel more comfortable sending a greeting card, don't just sign your name; handwrite a personal note in ink inside the card in complete sentences, with a salutation and signature. It's still not nearly as comforting as a real handwritten note, but it's much better than just a card.

3. Do send thanks within a week and sympathy within a month. Strive to be prompt, but don't just give up if you have already let it slide: Late is still a hundred times better than never.

4. Do return to the sender, with a gentle note, any letter that you think they regret having sent you. It's the only humane thing to do (see No. 7 above). Forgive them. Try to forget it came. And don't ever make that mistake yourself.

5. Do use your own stationery. Swiping hotel letterhead and envelopes to use at home, even as a joke, makes you look tacky. You wouldn't give the hotel's bathrobe or towels to someone as a gift, would you? You may use the stationery of any place you are staying if it is provided (and usually you may request it) while you are there.

6. When you send holiday cards to a dozen or a hundred of your closest friends, do include your writing inside or outside or both. Either handwrite the address on the envelope to create the initial impression that the greetings have been sent by a friend, or handwrite a message inside to dispel the suspicion, already created by a typed label, that it has been sent by a machine. (If you are very busy, it's better to spend your time on personal greetings than on hand addressing. But only you can judge what your friends and relations expect.) Rethink, and in some cultures don't even consider, sending any holiday cards that don't include your handwriting *somewhere*. If you're too busy to handwrite anything to your friends at holiday time, maybe you've let yourself get too busy. Send cards every second year, reduce your mailing list, have your family help out, or send a personalized "after Christmas" card in January, when you are less stressed.

7. Do use handwritten notes to humanize your business relationships, especially when people have done more than the occasion calls for. Add a handwritten line to a typed letter in addition to your signature, take the trouble to add more than a signature to your holiday greeting cards, and include a note with a corporate gift. Thank the colleague's spouse who had you to dinner at their house (and your own spouse, when you invite business people to dinner at your house!). If you thank a subordinate for something specific on the job, add a photocopy to their file.

NOT QUITE NOTES

The handwritten note lets you express who you are. If you choose instead to send something that is not quite the real thing, you will appear a little less courteous than you could be. Stop and think before you handicap yourself. These hybrids, clones, wanna-bes, and pseudo notes are often virtually as much trouble to write as real notes and deliver a lot less of a message, or even the wrong message.

Handwriting on a *preprinted form* such as a card store invitation implies that more than one person is receiving this same information. You communicate not one-to-one but in the role of the host for a group. This fill-in-the blanks approach is appropriate only for personal parties, where one person is sending to a small number. If you are over the age of four, don't fill in the blanks for a thank-you note.

A picture postcard, plain card, or folded *self-mailer* implies that the message is not quite private or important enough to de-

Bill Clinton adds a heartfelt sentiment to this
Mother's Day card for his grandmother.

serve an envelope. This may be appropriate, but keep in mind how easy it is to add warmth and class to the message you've handwritten by simply enclosing it in an envelope.

A printed *greeting card* is often a sincere attempt to acknowledge an occasion that the writer thinks is too important for their own words. But if the thought is that important, then your own words, no matter how plain, will be especially welcome. Always add your own handwritten words to the card you send.

If a card is expected—children and teenagers are particularly happy to get them if they're funny, older people may appreciate their ceremonial tone—then be sure you have added three things: salutation, text, and signature. Dear (Reader), I thought you might like this card; it reminded me of (something you both share). Best wishes (your signature). Write in complete sentences. Hand-address the envelope. And don't ever just send a printed greeting card without handwriting on it somewhere; that announces that you don't really want to connect. You might try a blank card with designs on the outside but space for your own words on the inside.

Counterfeit Materials, Handwriting, and Wording

Handwritten notes are valuable because they are so hard to fake. But that doesn't stop people from trying, either out of laziness, disorganization, or a real desire to trick you into reading their message.

Don't devalue the art of the handwritten note by misusing it yourself or responding to those who send pseudo-personalized mail. Follow these cautions:

Don't use your handwriting to address an envelope containing a letter written or signed by someone else. You may add a few personal words by hand on printed invitations (to people whom you know) for business or charity events you are involved in. Don't participate in chain letters. Don't photocopy your handwritten message with the intent to convince the reader that it is personal. Don't hand-address an envelope without attaching a signed note to whatever clipping, photograph, or form letter you enclose. If you are inviting someone to a personal event, don't automatically hire someone else, even a talented calligrapher, to address the envelopes. Your handwriting is you. Give it generously but give it honestly.

"While writing, the very

toil gives pleasure."

—OVID, 10 B.C.

IV

A Basic Recipe for

Writing Any Note

Now that you have chosen how to express who you are on paper, here is what should go into any note you write:

Write from a Space of Your Own

Set up a *note-writing place* that includes a chair, worktable or desk, and lamp. Leave everything set up and use it often. Assemble your materials: stationery, pen, address list, scratch paper, pencil, stamps. (Optional: a postage scale and a blotter to provide a smooth writing surface and protect the desktop.) If you can't leave your materials set up, gather them in a drawer or basket to keep them from wandering off when they are not in use.

If you like to write on your lap, set a board or big book on top of a pillow. If you work on the floor, prop your shoulders up with a pillow so your elbow doesn't get cramped. If you like to work at a stand-up desk, adjust it to the proper height.

Getting Started

Get comfortable: Adjust the chair to the right height, clear away surface clutter, smooth the writing surface, sit with good posture, support your elbow, provide good light. Silence the phone and other messaging hardware to minimize distractions, unless you can write notes during pauses in your e-mail and phoning. Be sure you have a view or a focus point to look at. Soothe all your senses with background music, fragrances, tea or coffee, and other small comforts.

If you have a special place and a simple ritual, it will help you develop the habit of writing. But if you are good at changing gears during your day, you could try to carry notes with you to make use of those chunks of wasted time when you could write—waiting in the doctor's office or airport lounge, sitting around on hold.

You may want to address the envelope before you write the note, to prompt your imagination to visualize the reader in a real space. Look at the note from them, or their picture, or the gift, or the announcement, or anything else that prompts you to write. Think about the person you are writing to. Picture the two of you sitting in a familiar coffeeshop or bar, or at your kitchen table, or in a dorm lounge, telling about the interesting small details in your day, sharing important news, asking a question, or offering a helpful idea to each other. A note can catch that moment and put it on paper.

Here is the basic format for a handwritten note, with some choices you can make about alternate elements, in an imaginary note to Alexandra Murray, written by Frederick Stanton, on February 6, 2001, to thank her for the gift of a book of crossword puzzles.

Place. Des Moines. Or: 4321 Grand Avenue, Des Moines, Iowa 50000. Use the city name at the very least. Your full address can go here or at the end; you may abbreviate the state. Include the zip code if you think the person will respond to this note and doesn't have your full address.

Date. Europeans and Americans write dates with slightly different formats. Or you can write the date out.

American date: 2, 6, 2001 or *February 6, 2001*

European date: 6, 2, 2001 or *6 February 2001*

The 6th of February 2001 or *The sixth day of February, two thousand one*

Salutation. Use a title and various parts of the person's name to signal more or less formality, more or less intimacy.

Dear Alexandra: When in doubt, use the whole first name.

Dear Sandy: Use a nickname only if you are certain that the person likes it (she may prefer Alex or Lexa or something else) and that you are entitled to that degree of intimacy and informality.

Dear Toad: Don't use childish nicknames if the person may prefer to have outgrown them; do use them if it's a special relationship you share.

Dear Mr. (Mrs., Miss, Ms.) Dr. Murray: Use social titles if there is a big difference in age or social status, to show more formality and less intimacy. Get the titles right: Academics often prefer the inverse snobbery of Mr. or Ms. instead of using their Dr. (for doctor of philosophy) title. Be sure an older woman isn't going to be offended by your use of Ms. if she has strong opinions about its use.

Dear Alexandra Murray: Appropriate only for business casual and unlikely to be used in a handwritten note.

Dear Aunt Alexandra, Dear Grandma Murray, Dear Grandma Sandy, My dear cousin: Use kinship titles with grown-ups' names until you are on an equal footing with your relative—if you ever catch up!

Dear Mom, Mother: Use a kinship title by itself for unique kinship.

My dear, Dearest lover, Honey, Snookums: Some terms of endearment that you use in speech can carry over to writing.

Hello, Hello, Alex: an import from e-mail that suits many brief and friendly notes.

Hi, Alex, yo!, Well: very informal greetings from verbal culture.

Text. Three sentences are a minimum and will fill one side of a notecard nicely. It is abrupt to start with "Thank you" but unnecessary to pad your first sentence with "I write to say" or "Well" or "This note is to say." You can start with *I,* or find short phrases to guide the reader into your message: "I was so pleased to," "You were so nice to," "What a nice surprise," "That was a thoughtful gift," "It was a treat when we," etc. Try to phrase positive thoughts with positive words, i.e., be glad, not terribly glad or awfully glad, and say I had a wonderful time rather than I've never had a better time.

:) *Emoticons.* Any reader under thirty will have no problem interpreting these typographic inventions retranslated back into handwriting and rotated ninety degrees. (Hint: To read, put your left ear on your left shoulder.) Don't rule out these emigrants from e-mail, along with predigital glyphs like smiley faces and acronyms like LOL, XXOO, and SWAK (acronyms for laughing out loud, kisses and hugs, sealed with a kiss). They are standard usage for many young writers and readers.

Use a *windup phrase* like "thank you again" or "looking forward to seeing you soon" to make a gracious transition to the complimentary closing and then your signature. This last sentence of the main text is the written equivalent of the small talk, change in tone of voice, throat clearing, and changes in posture that you would naturally use in a real conversation to prepare your listener for your farewell gesture.

Closing. The complimentary closing is the equivalent of whatever farewell you would give in person—the words you choose can create the impression of a wave, handshake, hug, or kiss.

Cheers, Bye, So long, Ciao, Regards, All the best=Wave
(breezy, impersonal)

Sincerely, Sincerely yours, With best regards=Handshake
(impersonal, formal)

Yours, Yours truly, Truly yours, Very truly yours=Hug
(personal, casual)

Affectionately, Fondly, All my love, Love, Your own=Kiss
(very personal)

Other closings have specific overtones:

Yours in Christ, Under the glory: Use only when your religious well-wishing will be welcome to the other person.

Your loving sister, your faithful friend, your doting mother: These very specific, personal closings let you sign your name without or instead of your kinship title.

Your obedient servant: antiquated. Use only if the note is to be presented on a silver tray, by a white-gloved butler to someone in a mansion.

Your closing is positioned on a separate line, starting halfway between the right and left margins. Capitalize the first word of the closing and follow the last word with a comma; then drop down one more line and sign your name.

Signature. You will sign most handwritten notes with your first name. If you have any particular title you would like the person to use, enclose it in parentheses after your name to help them when they reply. You do not usually sign your name with the title in front. Thus, if Aunt Alexandra is writing to invite her grand-niece's friends to lunch, she might make it easy for the young person to reply by putting Miss, Mrs., or Dr. in parentheses after her name—otherwise the young person can logically guess that addressing her by Ms. will not offend her.

If you greeted the person with their first name, you should sign your first name; if you greeted them with an old nickname, you'd better sign off with yours. (No fair greeting your friend as "Dorkbutt" if you are going to sign yourself "W. Framley Fenster, Jr."!)

Aunt Alexandra can drop her kinship title and sign off as just Alexandra, and even Mom can use her real name as her children get older, to remind them that relatives have real identities beyond their relationship to their offspring.

If you'd like to be on a first-name basis with an older or more formal person, greet them with their title and last name but sign your first name. Older people sometimes like to wait until they know you before they invite you to use their first name.

Postscript (after writing). You may add your phone or fax number, or e-mail address, under your signature to prompt your reader to reply this way to your note. This makes it easy for them to respond.

P.S.: Keep postscripts to one sentence.

P.P.S. More than two postscripts in a note, like more than two encores in a concert, start to seem gushy and artificial. Just write another note tomorrow.

And if you realize on the way to the mailbox that you forgot something important, you can write it, small, on the outside of the envelope; but remember that this breathless afterthought will be the first thing they read, not the last.

Envelope

A well-addressed envelope will get the note to the reader without delay, keep its contents private, and set up a pleasant sense of anticipation for what is inside. Strive for clarity and grace.

Curiously enough, the hallmark of a real handwritten note is the envelope, and though many ingenious shortcuts have been invented, you can send a clear message that your words are worth reading by putting the note into a hand-addressed envelope and sticking full postage on it. Your handwritten note deserves an envelope the way a homemade cake deserves frosting; the fact that you don't technically need it doesn't mean that people don't like to find it there.

If you are uncertain about what title a woman would prefer, here are some guidelines to inspire your guesswork. Use Ms. if a married woman has kept her name, Mrs. if she uses her husband's name. Older and more traditional women may prefer to be addressed with not only Mrs. but their husband's first and last name, that is, Mrs. Gordon Murray, not Mrs. Alexandra Murray (which to some people is the configuration of a divorced woman's name). Your aunt may seem like Alexandra Murray to you but she may in fact prefer to receive mail addressed to Mrs. Gordon Murray, even after the death of Gordon Murray himself.

Return address, including zip code. You can omit your name if you give it in full in the note or the person is very familiar with who you are. Return address stickers are convenient for all but the most formal envelopes; many organizations send them free as a fund-raiser. Return address can be on front or back, although the post office prefers it on the front.

Address: Layout can be flush left or slanted left. Use the person's or couple's titles the way you think they would prefer. If couples have different last names, write both their names in full on separate lines.

The *stamp* must be in the upper right corner. It can be seasonally appropriate or color-coordinated.

Back of envelope: Prestigious store or brand-name embossing give subtle clues to quality. An envelope with contrasting lining inside is more elegant and also more opaque.

Creative touches: Matching or contrasting envelope paper, matching stamp decor, colored ink, stickers, decorative return address stickers, rubber stamps, larger size, glitter. Invent your own airmail edging stripes and "Airmail" lettering.

PUSHING THE ENVELOPE

Balance your need to express yourself with the mail carrier's need to read the address by confining decoration to the name of the addressee or the edges of the envelope. Any nonstandard addressing risks delay, damage, or misdelivery. If your envelope is a nonstandard size or thicker than 1/4″ write "hand cancel" on the outside. If you have any doubt about how much postage is needed, check with the post office. Nothing smaller than 5″ by 3″ can be sent in the mail. (This rules out those small valentines that children routinely exchange in school.)

A very decorative, delicate, tiny or valuable envelope, with the recipient's name only, can be enclosed in an outer envelope—a traditional custom for formal weddings—or just delivered by hand.

"As cold water is to a thirsty

soul, so is good news

from a far country."

—PROVERBS 25:25

V

Opportunities to Write the
Note That Counts

Daily life offers many opportunities to use the pen and paper you have chosen with so much care. You may start by writing the notes you have to, but discover immediately that the handwritten note can get to be habit forming. It's fun to write and impressive to receive, and people respond to it. What seems at first like an obligation quickly becomes an opportunity, and you may find yourself actually looking for occasions to put your words on paper.

People are not born knowing instinctively exactly what words to choose; they have looked them up in books like this one for at least two hundred years. A century ago, a young man with a crush would consult a manual of letter writing to find out how to pen a declaration of love, and the mother of his beloved might consult the same manual to find out how to invite him to pay a call. One manual even helps a young lady compose a polite request for a suitor to direct his affections somewhere else! A Victorian father about to give advice could turn to a dozen models of sage counsel, diplomatically worded. Letters of complaint, letters of recommendation, letters of invitation—all were written with the aid of established models of handwriting script and prescribed forms of wording.

While some letters still follow models, most aspects of life have gotten more informal, and the telephone and the World Wide Web have changed many social customs and simplified many social forms. But one thing has not changed; written language offers the opportunity to say the right thing, but it also contains the danger of getting it wrong. And it doesn't have to be very wrong to be wrong; if, for instance, your note vaguely thanks your cousin for "the gift," he may quite legitimately suspect that you can't remember what it was. As Mark Twain said, "The difference between the right word and the wrong word is the difference between the lightning . . . and the lightning bug." Chintzy materials, careless handwriting, misspelled words, or insincere phrases can make your whole note a little off key, and while your readers will probably still be happy to hear from you, they may not get the message you think you've sent. So look at the handwritten mail you receive, and study the examples given in this book, to learn how to say just what you mean.

Turn Speech into Script

 Each time you write a note by hand, you put on paper primal human emotions: gratitude, sympathy, regret, gregariousness, affection, or nostalgia. You phrase these emotions with some of the very first, finest words every human learns to say, the bedrock of civilization: thank you, I'm sorry, come over, please, I love you, wow!, and guess what! Each section in this chapter helps you transform your best emotions into speech, and speech into script.

December 2, 02

Dear Cora,

We enjoyed the evening with you and your cousins so much! It was a pleasure to talk to someone just back from the kind of Italian trip we want to take next year. And your risotto was perfect. Thank you for taking so much time and trouble for us.

Yours,
Marion

Thank You

Saying thank-you is what prompts most people to start writing notes. Expressing gratitude is not an obligation; in fact, it is one of the most intense pleasures you can have. Your thank-you note should recapture the smile and handshake or hug you would give the giver in person, and offer it in a form that can be read and reread. Although there are many ways to say thank you on paper, the best kind of thank-you note has five key characteristics: *generous, specific, prompt, succinct, and personal:*

Five Characteristics of a Good Thank-You Note:

Generous. *Send a note* even if you've already thanked the giver another way.

Specific. *Mention the gift* but thank them for the thought behind it.

Prompt. *Send the note right away,* but don't let lateness stop you from writing at all.

Succinct. *Keep it short* by writing about any unrelated matters in a separate note.

Personal. *Write it by hand.* No form letters, printout, or greeting cards.

People will give you gifts throughout your life that make you feel grateful. From a baby rattle to a retirement watch, the reasons for giving are the same; somebody thought of you and wanted to feel connected to you. They took the time, trouble, and expense to let you know that they care about you. Even if you have also thanked them in person or some other way, you must write that thank-you note and send it promptly. This completes your connection with them that they began with their gift to you. William James said, "What people truly crave is appreciation," and when they read your note they will feel truly appreciated.

BASIC PHRASES TO ANCHOR YOUR THANK-YOU NOTE

Do Say:

Thank you so much

It's just what I've always wanted

How did you guess I wanted a [the gift]

I was just wishing for [name of gift]

I can't wait to use it [specifics]

I am enjoying wearing, playing with, looking at, eating, listening to, reading [the gift]

We are having fun using [the gift]

You've made a big difference to me

You were so thoughtful, kind, generous

I am so grateful to you

I was so pleased

We enjoyed the evening

Don't Say:

Thank you for the gift [If you do not mention the gift specifically by name in the note, it implies that you have lost the gift or forgotten what they gave you.]

You shouldn't have

Thank you for dinner

I'm exchanging it

It's the greatest thing I've ever received [Exaggeration reeks of insincerity.]

KINDS OF GIFTS

Although it is important to thank the giver in the context of the occasion, your thank-you note is also based partly on the gift itself. Different gifts can call for thank-you notes with different materials, script, and phrasing. Gifts can be things, money, or actions, or some combination of all three; furthermore, the things you receive may be permanent or perishable or somewhere in between. Your note can be tailored to the gift.

The most permanent gifts, for example, are household objects like china, linens, crystal, silver, classic books, and art, and personal treasures like a watch, jewelry, or a fountain pen, as well as semipermanent large appliances and cars. The thank-you notes for these expensive gifts must reassure the giver that you appreciate the enduring value of the object and will take good care of it, in addition to appreciating the importance of the occasion and the kindness of the thought behind the gift. Use very formal stationery.

Less expensive, less permanent presents are intended to last a year or two, like subscriptions, calendars, plants, paperbacks, clothing, perfume, and stationery. The implicit message is that this gift is to be used up and worn out. Your thank-you should take note of the gift's usefulness and appropriateness, and emphasize how it will continue to remind you of the giver throughout the year. If the gift and the occasion—a magazine subscription at Christmas, for instance—hold the possibility for annual renewal, the wording of your note can hold that door open or tactfully close it. The stationery should be less formal.

Inexpensive, temporary gifts are chosen purposely to fade or go out of date all on their own; they use themselves up fast, without much effort from you. People give flowers, candy, and wine—on many specific occasions or just to send a message of their own. Built-in obsolescence makes them a generous gesture. Your thank-you should include recognition of that gesture and the impulse behind it. Use casual stationery and wording to respond to a casual gift at the same level.

Some occasions inspire people to give you a gift, but they

don't know what you would like. The thank-you note you write when you've been given cash or a check or a gift certificate should tell the giver some very specific information. Try to come up with something definite you can say you used it for (or plan to use it for) that will give you especial happiness and remind you of the giver's generosity.

Many gifts come in the form of time, effort, patience, information, and hospitality from people who act out of generosity. These intangibles deserve handwritten thank-you notes too.

If, as often happens, you receive a perishable gift as a thank-you for an intangible, you have the option to write a less formal thank-you for a thank-you. Don't keep the volley going back and forth too long, however; a bouquet of flowers that arrives to thank you for a dinner party doesn't require a note, while a bouquet of flowers from your coworkers that arrives at your hospital bed does require a note.

Send thank-you notes promptly for gifts that come in the mail from far away, to let the sender know that the gift arrived safely. If the package arrives long before you are going to open it, you should e-mail, phone, or fax the person just to let them know it arrived and that you are happily looking forward to opening it. This takes a little pressure off the transaction but does not substitute for a real handwritten note.

Send thank-you notes just as promptly, however, to people in your neighborhood or workplace so that you can meet them without feeling defensive and apologetic. Informal thank-yous in a variety of written formats can be "delivered" immediately in creative ways to the pillows, mirrors, steering wheels, or computer screens of the people in your house.

SPECIFIC OCCASIONS
FOR GIFTS AND THANKS

Most gifts will be given to you on special occasions that are predictable. Since you know ahead of time that you are likely to receive gifts, you don't have to get caught napping by the need for thank-you notes; you can be prepared to do the right thing—with pens and stationery, addresses and stamps, handwriting and wording. A little planning will let you look forward with pleasure, not panic, to what is after all the opportunity to make someone happy who has just made you happy. Read about these annual, occasional, or once-in-a-lifetime occasions, when gifts will offer you the opportunity for expressing gratitude with a handwritten note.

ANNUAL HOLIDAY

You probably exchange Christmas, Hanukkah, or Kwanzaa gifts with family and friends to celebrate the December holiday season. Holiday thank-you notes have the special dimension of reciprocity. Because virtually everyone in the Americas, Europe, Australia, and Japan is both giving and receiving gifts at this time of year, you can participate in both sides of the experience—*the warmth you feel when you read a thank-you note written to you is the flip side of the happiness the thank-you note you write brings someone else.* You can remind yourself, whenever you receive a note, how welcome your note will be.

Thank-you notes for holiday business gifts can be sent to the giver's home or workplace, depending on how the gift itself was delivered. An e-mail or a word in the hallway for a small informal or impersonal holiday gift or card from someone at work may be appropriate, and is certainly better than no response at all. But in a business setting a note, which can be circulated and posted—may mean more than a verbal phrase or a purchased gift.

> January 8, 01
>
> Dear Melanie,
>
> I want to thank you for the annual box of candy that INK INC so generously sends to my team. They appreciate the chocolates, the gesture, and the creative printwork you do for us all year. Thank you all and Happy New Year.
>
> Sincerely,
> Andrew Long

You and the person you exchange holiday gifts with deserve to receive thank-you notes from each other. One gift does not "cancel out" the other, but creates an opportunity for both people to express their gratitude for a shared friendship. In a way, the gifts themselves are not as important in your friendship as the thank-you notes that result.

Some holiday gifts may come from people far away; because they may be wondering if the gift got there at all, your note should be extra prompt. This may be your annual chance to stay in touch, so it's worth the care to get it right.

Some holiday gifts may come from people close to you, whom you see often. But even if you open the gifts together, thank each other later on paper. The notes you write to your own children or younger relatives are perhaps the most important of all, because you can inspire them to write their own notes.

ANNUAL BIRTHDAY OR ANNIVERSARY

The gifts you receive every year on your birthday or anniversary celebrate the passage of time and your uniqueness as a person. As with holiday gifts, you don't have to do anything to earn these gifts, just survive (or help your marriage survive) for one more year. Although these annual events focus on you, your thank-you note enlarges the spotlight to shine also on the generosity of your friends.

In general, people you invite to a celebration will assume a gift is appropriate and then they will legitimately expect a thank-you note. You may also want to thank them just for attending the party itself. While you plan the party, plan on writing notes afterward.

Party or no party, birthday gifts require a thank-you note written by you in your own handwriting. "Fred says thank-you for the Ferrari," is acceptable only if the car is two inches long and Fred is still in diapers. Anniversary gifts can be acknowledged by either member of the couple.

MILESTONES: COMING OF AGE, GRADUATING, MARRYING, RETIRING

You are likely to receive major gifts that require thank-you notes at once-in-a-lifetime events. Presents often come from people who have been invited to, or notified of, this kind of celebration. As you grow up, you pass milestones other than birthdays that mark your progress into adult social life. Your family and friends arrange parties and give you gifts to show how happy they are to see you grow up. As an emerging adult, you begin to realize how much love and time and money have gone into these parties and gifts, and you look for ways to show your gratitude. *A handwritten thank-you note is the best way not only to show this gratitude but also to demonstrate this new maturity.* Gifts given to celebrate your coming of age, given most often by people who knew you when you were a child, must be acknowledged with the kind of graceful thank-you note worthy of your new adult status. This is a good time to outgrow kids' stationery, pencil scribbles, excuses, lateness, bad grammar, and misspellings. Your note can be informally worded, but write it neatly on stationery that is not too cute, to show that you know it is not an obligation nor a joke.

Marriage is a major milestone in every culture around the world. You can expect the most significant gifts, intended to endure for a lifetime, when you have a wedding, in recognition of your new status as a family and your need to set up an adult household. A prompt thank you is especially important to let the giver know that a valuable gift has arrived safely; fine stationery and penmanship pay tribute to the importance of the occasion;

Thank you so much.
The invitations are
beautiful!
Jim

Dear Aunt Margaret,
    Thank you so much for the
sublime effort on our behalf in
crafting the invitation for our
wedding. It is utterly gorgeous
and is a huge honor.
                    Love,
                      Helen

gracious wording tells them that you appreciate what is in their hearts as much as what was in the box. Enclosures like a photo or clipping are a nice touch.

Getting married also may include a cluster of small durable *engagement, shower,* and *attendants'* gifts, as well as special gifts traditionally given by the bride and groom to each other. Thank-you notes that are not strictly necessary are still important, even written later on, to mark the importance of the celebration. People who have been verbally thanked for their gifts and for their help with arrangements should be thanked eventually on paper too. If any professional help was particularly good, let them know with a note too. And thank your clergyperson.

A *good-bye party* given in your honor may leave you feeling grateful to a group of people for a variety of gifts, favors, and arrangements. Similarly, whether your employer or your friends arrange your *retirement* party, you can figure out someone to thank on paper for gifts, toasts, and the party itself, and ask that your thank-you note be circulated or posted.

GRATITUDE FOR INTANGIBLES

Handwritten notes are not only for the kind of gifts that come wrapped up in a box. You should be alert to the many occasions when you can thank people who give you their time, their thoughts, their patience, their information, their connections, and their hospitality. These generous acts may surround an annual event or milestone, or occur throughout your life. A thank-you note can "repay" a person who takes you into their home, who arranges a party for you, who interviews you for a job, who writes a recommendation for you, who helps you campaign, who visits your sick relative, who sends you a letter of condolence.

You especially need to thank people who have given you their most personal gift, hospitality. If you share a meal at the home of a friend, relation, or coworker, you should send a thank-you note. If you sleep over in someone's house, you must send a thank-you note.

Only a generation ago, no one slept over in someone else's house without first being invited and then afterward sending a bread-and-butter letter to thank the host for the room and meals. Young people who turn up casually for meals and sleep over with their friends should try to see it from the point of view of the adults in the house and find some way to thank their friends' parents for hospitality.

HI JOE'S MOM AND DAD,
    JOE SAID IT WAS OK TO STAY. THANKS FOR THE BREAKFAST, TOO. You guys are COOL.
                          MIKE

Most of the occasions you have read about so far, of course, may include a friend or group of friends from your workplace, subordinates, or your boss, who will give you similar gifts but for somewhat different reasons. The thank-you notes you write to people whom you know only in the workplace will be similar to those you write to your family and friends but the tone will be more impersonal.

November 16, 2000

Dear Margaret —

Am hoping you will email me for a lunch date, but just received the list of recent donors and there you are. Many, many thanks. I am eager to bring you up to date — so many good things are happening. We've raised $8 million so far for the visual arts building. Another

Gifts and favors that are strictly *business* should be acknowledged with notes of a businesslike tone and appearance. Gifts to teachers from *students* offer an opportunity for the teacher to show young people how nice it is to receive an old-fashioned thank-you note in the mail. Gifts and favors to your *nonprofit organization* require thank-you notes with a very special tone and timing, and the thank-you note in *politics* plays a role all its own.

You don't have to actually be part of an organization yet to receive gifts, especially intangibles, that require *business thank-you notes*. If you are applying for a job in an organization, admission to a school, or membership in a club, you should follow up with a short note carefully thanking your interviewers for their time. An entrepreneur should send handwritten thanks to the venture capital investor who looks at their business plan. You may also receive a grant or award from an organization; you should write to one person there in a form that can be posted, published, or circulated to everyone. Inversely, an organization you belong to may receive a *donation* of time or money from an individual for which you should express thanks with a thank-you note in your own hand that speaks for your whole group as an organization.

WRITING AS SOMEONE ELSE'S THANKSPERSON

You may find yourself, as you grow up, expressing gratitude not only for gifts given to you but also for gifts that have been given to someone else. You may write as half of a couple, as a parent of a child, as a member of a family, as an employee of a company, or as a spokesperson for a group.

Vicarious gratitude, which adds an extra layer of thanks, often starts with wedding gifts and continues with thank-you notes for the baby gifts given at showers, baptismal parties, and

> Dear Michael & Tricia...   January 2001 ♡
>
> Thank you so much for thinking of me and my recent arrival into this world. The baby photo album is adorable, and my mom already has it displayed on my shelf.
>
> We loved having you visit & pretty soon I'll be coming over to play with Scout!!
>
> Love Daniel

the first five birthdays. You write these as the parent, acknowledging your gratitude for gifts given to your children, until the children learn to write for themselves. Most people who have had babies themselves will forgive you if your thank-you notes take the form of a personal phone call or e-mail (though a few people may feel that if they managed it, you can), and they will probably cut you some slack if you are slow in getting organized to mail a handwritten note. But they still need to know that the gift arrived safely, and they will probably like a photo of the baby (or a picture of the mother and the baby, since all newborn babies look the same in photographs).

Gifts given at a baby shower before the baby's birth should be acknowledged promptly, while you are still in control of your schedule. You're going to have your hands full soon. A box of notes, a sheet of decorative postage stamps, and an inexpensive fountain pen make a perfect shower gift for an expectant mother and father.

Gifts that celebrate the arrival of your baby are your opportunity to share your happiness and hopes with someone who will be interested in your child for years to come. Don't miss the opportunity to celebrate together and keep that connection warm.

Not every gift marks a celebration. Your loved ones can receive gifts when the thank-you notes you write on their behalf may be the only really happy element in the whole situation. If someone close to you is *ill* or *injured*, or *overwhelmed* by some catastrophe, you may need to intercept, look after, and thank people for gifts and actions. As soon as the patient can cope with daily life, you can hand the task back, organized, complete with lists and writing supplies, because the act of expressing gratitude has a strong therapeutic effect of its own and may actually help make them feel better.

Perhaps the ultimate note on behalf of someone else is the

thank-you note you write in response to the condolence note that comes after the *death* of someone close to you. You may feel too overwhelmed to respond to condolence notes at all; you may want to acknowledge them with a printed card in the mail or an announcement in the newspaper. See Chapter V for the reasons behind the custom of writing personal notes to acknowledge condolence letters. Many people who have survived the death of a loved person will tell you that handwriting a reply comforted them as much as it thanked the original sender. Saying thank-you is good for you even if your heart is broken. Expressing thanks for sympathy is a healthy part of the grieving process and a way to heal a web that may be weakened when a loved one dies.

Gifts come to you all through your life. Figure it out at about forty a year: baby presents at showers and birth, a bunch on each of your own birthdays plus party favors from others' birthdays, a basket from the Easter bunny, at least eight at Hanukkah, a stockingful from Santa and a heap under the Christmas tree, dozens at your confirmation, several graduations, bar mitzvah, or wedding . . . it adds up! And that's just the gifts you can see! By the time you reach twenty-five, you've probably received a thousand and one gifts—from your parents, your friends, your relatives, your coworkers, and a host of other people in your life who wish you well. As you learn to write thank-you notes to all 1001 of them (maybe even 1002: Be sure to thank your mom on your own birthday) you'll begin to realize that the person who feels happiest when that note gets written is you.

(Some of the suggestions here can also make writing thank-you notes easier for a foreign visitor to America, an unwell or injured person, or anyone else having trouble getting started.)

If you can teach your toddler to say thank-you out loud, you can teach your child to write a thank-you note. Children who have learned to write thank-you notes have an extra advantage as they go through life because people who happen to help them once will tend to keep helping them. The earlier they start writing notes, the more they will get the kind of positive feedback

> Dear Margaret
> Thank you for
> the Advent
> calendars. I like
> coloring the Black
> and white one.
> love, Sebastian

that encourages them to write again. Try a combination of the tactics described here:

1. *Schedule.* Children function better if they know what to expect and when it will happen. Set up, in advance, an hour on a certain day—the day after the holiday or birthday, perhaps, for the sole purpose of writing thank-you notes. Let the child know that this is a time when you will help her get started, and then make sure that it happens. Children also like a specific place set aside for certain activities. Add to the sense of ritual with favorite music, friendly materials, or symbolic costumes (remember Jo, in *Little Women,* who always put on her writing hat to signal to herself and her family that "genius burns!").

2. *Clerical support.* Give the child basic stationery, stamps, and a pen. Wrap it up nicely as a gift. Or let the child choose her own, steering her to the appropriate paper, design, and size for her age and the occasion. Stationery with faint guidelines may be appropriate. Make sure the child has an address list. Often simply not knowing someone's last name or where someone lives is enough to make a child put off writing to them. An address book with the givers' names and addresses already in it is a wonderful gift to a young child. Or address the envelopes for her while she writes the notes.

3. *Sugar coating.* If your child likes stickers, rubber stamps, colored pens, printed designs, glitter, huge or

tiny envelopes, provide them to add fun to the note-writing activity.

4. *Training wheels.* Children strive to master skills as they grow. But sometimes they need an intermediate step that breaks down the skill into manageable parts. Very young children may find it easier to dictate while they watch you transform what they say into handwriting; or they may enjoy copying a few phrases you have written out for them. Let the child take over the whole task as she gets older, more confident, and more experienced.

5. *Vicarious experience.* A child won't be motivated to master a grown-up social skill if he doesn't see a grown-up doing it. Model the behavior you want the child to learn. Let the child see how you say thank-you in person. Then let him see how that gratitude gets phrased and translated into a handwritten note. Pretend, if necessary, that you really enjoy writing it; at least don't grouse about it. And make sure he sees how you enjoy receiving thank-you notes from others. Read them out loud, pass them around, post them.

6. *Companionship.* Sit with the child and write something too: a journal, an assignment, your own thank-you notes. It's very helpful to the child just to have you there, ready to help with advice, addresses, spelling, and phrasing. Just knowing that she can ask for help will help her stick with the task.

7. *Practice*. Sometimes children—and adults—have trouble getting started simply because they are out of practice. Set them up to practice the exercises in this book. Encourage them to write things by hand all week long: lists, notes, a journal, doodling with a pen.

8. *Reward*. Some children work best when their only reward is their own satisfaction with a job well done. For other children, that isn't quite enough. If your child needs a reward, try something special that isn't just a simple bribe. A coupon for an intangible privilege, a token, or even a real thank-you note from you. If your child works better with some negative reinforcement, enforce the rule that the new toy or treat stays in view but out of reach until the note is written.

9. *Imaging*. Here and now is all a child knows. A child's imagination needs help recalling her own past emotions and picturing other people's feelings. Focus the child's memory by having the gift in sight nearby. Recall the fun she had opening it. Remind her of how she is going to enjoy using the gift or playing with the toy. If she didn't get particularly excited about that practical sweater from Grandma, help her imagine the goodwill that Grandma certainly felt in picking out the gift for her.

10. *Reciprocity*. Children have a hard time imagining other people's feelings because their own feelings occupy almost all their attention. Help your child understand the pleasure people get from being thanked by making sure

he himself knows what it feels like to give a gift and then receive a thank-you note. When a child gives you a gift, you have a "teachable moment." If he gets a real hand-written note of thanks from you, he'll understand vividly how his own thank-you notes bring happiness to some-one else. At some ages, he may even like to watch you write and mail it! All adults should make a special extra effort to send a handwritten note to thank a child for any kind of gift or gesture, and share the notes they receive from others.

When you give a gift to a child, a bride, a traveler, a new par-ent, a socially inexperienced person, or a person with a disadvan-tage, make it easy for them to write a thank-you note: Include your whole name, clearly spelled, with your mailing address. Don't come down too hard on them if they are late. It's a teach-able moment, when you can help them do the right thing. Ask them in the meanwhile if the gift got there; say that you hope it fits or pleased them; tell them that you'd love to hear from them. If you've given them every sweet opportunity to respond, the ball's in their court.

Q&A

I opened a present in front of the giver. I loved the gift and thanked them warmly for their thoughtfulness. Do I still owe them a thank-you note?

Yes. You have been given, in addition to the gift itself, the opportunity to thank the giver for their generosity in a form they can read and reread at their leisure. A verbal thank-you can get lost in the chaos of the occasion. A note lets the giver know for sure that you really appreciate their efforts. If you wonder whether you owe them a note and decide you can get away with not writing it, perhaps next year they'll wonder whether they owe you a gift and decide they can get away with not giving it. And your connection with them will have been diminished.

If you open twenty birthday presents in front of twenty friends, each person has received only five percent of your attention. With a handwritten thank-you note, each person will feel one hundred five percent thanked and a few of them will be one hundred percent pleasantly surprised.

I appreciated the thought behind the gift but I really didn't like the gift. How do I phrase my note?

You can choose from three levels of truthfulness: frank, diplomatic, heroic. What you do depends on the occasion, on your connection with the giver, and on the giver's personality.

Frank. You may be able to write a thank-you note that frankly states that you loved the gift but can't use it the way it is—for example, a shirt that is too small or a book you already own. You can exchange it yourself for the right size (or perhaps for something else) or ask the giver first and thank them for the final result plus the thought behind it.

Diplomatic. You may also want just to tactfully thank the giver for the gift and not mention that you cannot use it; then you can exchange it or give it away without saying anything further to the giver about it.

Heroic. Once in a while, to spare the feelings of the giver completely, you must not only send prompt, handwritten thanks for the gift and keep the gift but also go through the motions of loving it and using it. It is masochism in the service of tact. You can learn to make this effort for those people—your own toddler or your great-aunt Susie—whose feelings you have decided are more important than yours.

I stay over at my buddy's house every second week. He stays over at my house on the other week. Why do I have to thank his mom? We're even.

You owe his mom a thank-you note because when you go to someone's house (unless you are Goldilocks) you are grateful for the same bed, blankets, TV, and refrigerator you take for granted at home. If you send or leave behind a thank-you note, even one that bunches together your thanks for several sleepovers, you will look spectacularly grown-up in their eyes and so, by reflection, will your buddy, their son. Thank-you notes are not something formal and artificial; they are part of an ongoing dialogue.

I've been given a generous, valuable, almost overwhelming gift. A thank-you note just doesn't seem like enough. What's the next step up?

Two thank-you notes, one immediately to say how over-whelmed you are, and another shortly thereafter, repeating your gratitude and adding some more thoughts about what this means to you now and for the future. There are also many ways to say thank-you in addition to writing it. After you've written to say how thrilled you are and how generous the giver is, you can follow up with something you've bought, written, made, or done.

THANK-YOU TOKENS

Write: poem, quotation
Buy: flowers/plant, candy, balloons
Make: photograph, certificate
Do: pay a visit, bake a cake, offer your time

Won't it look like trying to curry favor if I send thank-you notes to peo-ple who are famous, powerful, and rich when they've done something that's a big deal for me but probably not much to them?

You'd be surprised how pleased an important person can be to receive a simple courtesy. If you're uncertain of their response, use conventional stationery, simple phrasing, and clear handwrit-ing. Sign your whole name. Avoid phrases like "You don't know me but . . ." and "P.S. While you're at it, my kid wants your au-tograph."

My dinner guests each brought a gift—flowers, wine, cheese, and candy. Do I send thank-you notes for the gifts even though they haven't written to thank me for the dinner?

In general, no, and especially not if they have not written to you. In their minds, clearly, you're even. If a houseguest brings a gift but doesn't write a bread-and-butter letter, you don't have to write them a thank-you note for the gift. But you might help them come to their senses if you do.

I'm in charge of volunteers for the annual fund-raising event at my children's school. Do I write thank-you notes to people who gave their time, merchants who donated items, sponsors who gave money? They all got thanked in print in the program and thanked onstage at the event.

You should be sending those notes as fast as you can write, to everyone you can think of, on the nicest stationery you can find. You don't want to do all that work, donate all that stuff, and contribute all that money yourself next year, do you? You went into volunteer work not just to do the job of raising money but to nurture a network of support for your organization. The thank-you note is one of the small strands that strengthens and beautifies the fabric of everyday life.

I procrastinated about my thank-you notes and now they're a month late! I feel awful. I'm avoiding people because they're all mad at me.

Bite the bullet. Just write the note. Even if you've let ten notes slide, it's going to take only an hour or two to write them, and when even the first one is done, you're going to feel a hundred times better than you do now. *Don't apologize for more than one sentence, at the end; thank-you notes to people are about their generosity, not your rudeness.* The giver is not mad at you, they're just wondering: is everything all right, did the gift get there, and did the thought behind it make you happy? Sure, you are a little late, but people are so happy to hear from you, they will forgive you most of the wait.

> *"Always remember that it is never wrong*
> *to write a thank-you note."*
>
> —EMILY POST'S ETIQUETTE

I'm Sorry

A handwritten note is the best way to let someone know you are sorry that something bad has happened. There are three major kinds of "sorry"—condolence when someone close has died, sympathy when a disaster has occurred, and apology when you have done something hurtful to them—and three major forms of note.

DEATH

It is very, very important to send a handwritten note on the occasion of someone's death. It is not just an obligation but also a

> Dear Sarella,
>
> I've just heard about Victor's death from George Michaels at Com Labs, and I want to let you know how very sorry I am. He was a delightful colleague and friend, and will be missed by all who knew him and relished his dry humor & kind heart
>
> Did I ever tell you about the

golden opportunity to help someone else while you deal with your own sense of loss. John Donne said, "Every man's death diminishes me; no man is an island," and your note can strengthen your connection with the recipient, softening their loneliness.

A note also recognizes in its formality the immense importance of the event. A life's end is a solemn moment; your personal attention and individualized response is the only acceptable way to show your respect. *Neither a telephone call nor e-mail nor printed greeting card can be a substitute for a handwritten note.* A personal visit (if your relationship is close), attending the services in person, and writing a note are by far the best ways to sympathize.

If you have not lived through the death of someone close to you, then you will need to imagine how your reader is feeling and what a note can do to comfort them. There are clearly defined stages of grief:* 1. Denial and isolation 2. Anger 3. Bargaining 4. Depression 5. Acceptance. While your note will help at any stage, it will be particularly helpful during the last two. And you can write more than once to try to let your feelings help with theirs.

You should handwrite a condolence note even if you see the person often, to remind them that you are there and thinking of them. It may sound like a cliché, but they need that reassurance on paper.

Death takes a lot of getting used to. The survivor may be plagued by an unreasoning fear that the person who died will be forgotten and that nobody cares. A handwritten note is the strongest healing defense against that fear. Your note can emphasize the way that relationships don't die just because a person dies. Be specific. Remind them why you considered their loved one special or tell a story they may not know. These memories are very welcome, both at the time and years later. Sometimes a good friend of the deceased can open up a whole different understanding of who someone was even if that person isn't particularly close to the survivors.

E-mail and telephone are often unavoidable when dealing with death. You may e-mail short condolences immediately if you think the person will be checking e-mail. A recent survey found that three out of four people in America think that e-mail condolences are not offensive; you must decide if your friend is in the remaining twenty-five percent who do not find it comforting and may actually feel hurt. But merely being "not downright rude" is really not enough; you should still follow up your e-mail within

*Elisabeth Kübler-Ross

three weeks with a handwritten note. If you have telephoned, you still must write, as the shock of the first few days may leave the person unable to remember even that you called during that time when their life was so torn up. Your note, in contrast, can be saved to be read when they feel ready, and reread to help them when they have moved on to the next stage of grief. Later they may feel able to respond to your note with a handwritten thank-you note of their own, a printed card, or a newspaper acknowledgment.

Grief is a lengthy process; it may be entirely appropriate for you to write more than once during the first year of their bereavement and to give them special support by writing during the season or near the exact date of the loss, and on specific holiday, birthday, and anniversary dates. Even if you don't hear back directly in response to your note, you can be confident that you have done the right thing; your note may be reread many years or decades later, giving comfort to the original recipient and offering insight for later generations.

Pay extra attention to the materials you use. If you think you will want to write at length, use letter-sized sheets; but even a short note is far better than a greeting card. Keep your stationery simple but not gloomy or stark; avoid lighthearted decorations but include any visual image that seems tranquil and comforting: printed flowers, texture, landscapes. If you knew the person in an official connection, use your organization's stationery to show that you express the condolences of a group of people. Later on, a photo or other enclosure may bring happy memories.

Write with the best materials and handwriting you can—it's the visual equivalent of putting on clothing that is appropriate to a funeral and shows that you are taking extra care with the person's feelings and honoring the memory of the person who died.

Stationery can be formal; your ink should be blue or brown, not severe black or unusual purple or green. If you are speaking formally for your group, or if your note is a formal memoir of the person, you may type the note or letter and sign it.

Writing condolence notes is much easier if you yourself have experienced the death of someone who mattered to you. Not only do you know how important it is to *simply send a handwritten note,* but you also know *what words to write, and a few words to avoid.* Just think about what you needed to hear. Try to recall specific words that people said or wrote to you that were most helpful.

BASIC PHRASES TO ANCHOR YOUR CONDOLENCE NOTE

Do Say:

I'm so sorry

We're going to miss him

I have so many wonderful memories of her

I hope you're doing okay; I will write again after the memorial service

I'm thinking of the nice time we all had together last summer

He had a wonderful life

I remember

I knew her through [connection]

We worked together

The [detail] of the services was so comforting

He would have loved [remembered vignette]

Can I help by [Offer something practical and specific like a guest room, picking up visitors, buying groceries, sorting the mail, walking the dog.]

Don't Say:

I didn't know him very well

It's awful

I'm so sad, I'm so upset

You must be devastated

The same thing happened to me, only worse

It's better this way

I don't know what to say

You can always have more children

At least you didn't have to [Don't try to second-guess what they would have preferred to the person's death if they'd had the choice.]

Life must go on

What can I do to help

I know how you feel

Don't Use Euphemisms

It is important to remember the power of pen and ink to make words real. Be sure you *write the name* of the person who died, and continue addressing a widow as Mrs. David Smith until the time when she may want to rearrange her name. Do not be squeamish about the words *dead, death,* and *die.* "Death is indeed a stark word," writes Nina Hartman Donelley, but tiptoeing around it with careful euphemisms or distancing it with tasteful greeting cards doesn't help the mourner deal with it. Seeing the words in your handwriting will help the reader (and you yourself) to move through the early denial stage of grieving, and ultimately to accept the reality of what happened.

A century ago, a person in mourning wrote all correspondence on special black-edged stationery for the first year of bereavement, and during that period also wore black clothing. (Widows wore only black; a relative could wear a black armband to signify distant bereavement.) As time passed, social custom allowed the black border to get thinner and thinner and the mourner to wear less and less black.

No other experience hurts as much as the death of a parent, spouse, sibling, or child, but everyone eventually suffers some form of bereavement. You can help express your sympathy and solidarity no matter how close or distant your relationship is. You will word your note a little differently based on whether you know both the person who died and the survivor, or you know only the person who died and not the survivor, or if you know only the survivor and not the person who died.

Death and its rituals may prompt you to send flowers, bring over gifts of food, sign a visitors' book, e-mail your travel plans, or telephone to offer help. These mean a lot. Combine your hand-written note with these other forms of communication if you like, but *write the note.* You may also be particularly useful to a friend or relative who needs help to organize the notes and letters and flowers and food and cards and contributions that come in. Keep all the mail in one file after it has been read and shared. Make it easy for them to respond, once they begin to recover, by keeping a list of who wrote and visited and phoned.

A passage from a book or a newspaper (not the kind printed on a greeting card) is a comforting enclosure. If you have calligraphic talents, one of the nicest condolence mementos can be the gift of a quotation hand-lettered by you; either the words of the person who died or a quotation that was a favorite of theirs. Simple lettering (or even neat typing), good paper, and an inexpensive mat from a photo shop can elevate this from a gesture into a treasure.

"Never think, because you cannot write a letter easily, that it is better not to write at all. The most awkward note imaginable is better than none."

—EMILY POST'S ETIQUETTE

A second kind of sympathy note offers your support to a friend or relative who is coping with some problem: illness, a difficult move, a parent in decline, a child in trouble, a theft, a fire, a public disgrace, a financial collapse, a divorce. Depending on the seriousness of the situation, a note from you supporting them through their bad luck may be the most helpful thing you can do. But promptness is everything—a get-well note after they're back on their feet will show your good intentions but won't really do them much good. Grab a pen, any pen, and write. And don't necessarily expect any written acknowledgment beyond knowing that you did the right thing.

The *get well* note has been largely engulfed by the get well card. But as with the condolence note, even though you may feel that a card says it better, you should add several complete sentences in your own handwriting. Or enclose a separate personal note with the card. Remember, the person probably has a lot of extra time to reread whatever you send and think good thoughts about you. For that reason, it's thoughtful to include a cartoon, puzzle, clipping, small artwork print, or poem.

OOPS

If you think it takes effort to write to a friend who has a problem, picture how hard it is when you're the one who has created the problem! The note that repairs a relationship after you have goofed is one of the hardest, most important, and, strangely, one of the most welcome notes you can learn to write. All the hard part comes up front—you have to admit to yourself what your role was in making the problem; find phrases to define, not overstate or understate the situation; apologize; and offer a way to repair the damage. Don't gloss over the importance of your mistake, but don't grovel.

A handwritten apology may be easier than a verbal apology and more effective when it arrives. If you write your apology by hand, it will seem warmer and less legalistic than a printed-out hand-signed letter. From losing a hammer to missing an anniversary, a note is almost always a better way to say I'm sorry. An e-mail apology is adequate only for very trivial errors; if you sincerely want forgiveness, you may just inflict further hurt by the impersonality of e-mail. It may be appropriate to send e-mail saying that a note is on its way. (That alone may accomplish some of the note's purpose and make someone more receptive to its message.)

Be very careful, however, about a written apology that could be held against you as evidence in some ongoing social dispute or in legal proceedings. If you are in any doubt, consult with a lawyer first and speak to the person face-to-face. If you write a note of apology to a litigious person, keep a photocopy.

PHRASES TO ANCHOR APOLOGY LETTERS

Do Say:

Please forgive me

I'm sorry

I apologize

Can you excuse my mistake

I hope you will understand

What can I do to make amends

I regret that this happened

Don't Say:

Oops

I am an idiot

Please let me pay

It wasn't my fault

You're probably mad about this

I don't know why you are so upset

Q&A

I am late writing a sympathy note, and I don't know what to say.

Condolence is so welcome that its lateness is not nearly as important as the fact that you wrote. You can write a note weeks and months after someone has lost a loved one: Send a card right away if you are at a loss for words, and then start to jot down things you can put into writing later. Don't apologize for being late. The dead person will still be dead and the living person will continue to feel pain for months and years to come.

I didn't know the person who died, but I know the survivor. I feel like I ought to write something. I don't want to intrude, but I don't want to look like I don't care.

Even if you didn't know your friend's parent, spouse, sibling, or child, it is important to write a note. Just three sentences can convey the simple words you would not hesitate to say in person. For instance: "I'm so sorry to hear about your dad. I remember all the times you said what a great guy he was. I bet you are able to be a great comfort to your mom. Best wishes from Beth and me; we're thinking of you and wish we could do something." There, now; it may be plain, but isn't that better than a greeting card with a picture of a flower and a printed verse?

I knew the person who died, but I don't know the surviving son. What can I say?

You can tell him something special that you shared with his dad. Condolence notes can help enlarge the picture that people have of their loved one, telling them things they didn't know or filling out sketchy memories. But beware of seeming to assert a special relationship with the deceased, adding to the survivor's feeling that something more is being taken away. Younger children are particularly uncomforted to hear other people claiming connection with the parent, who was their whole world and whom they subconsciously want to remember as belonging solely to them.

I wrote a sympathy note. I never heard anything back. Do you think I said the wrong thing and hurt their feelings? I don't know what to do next.

Right now you're feeling a little of what they feel: isolation, uncertainty, incompleteness. You did the right thing, but you may feel less confident about hand-writing your condolence notes, playing it safe in the future by sending a printed card or just doing nothing. This is why a thank-you for a condolence note is so important. If your note is not acknowledged, just be understanding and have confidence that you did the right thing.

I'm only ten years old. Do I have to write something to the lady who lives next door whose husband died? I don't know what to say to grown-ups.

Most grown-ups are human too; they feel sad and hurt when someone dies. They may be comforted even more by the kindness of a kid who writes a note because most kids can't imagine death and usually haven't experienced the death of someone they know well. If you're worried about your spelling or what to say, ask a parent or teacher. Don't let them discourage you by telling you it's okay not to write. Your first, kind instinct is the right one.

Dear Mrs. Friend,

I am very sorry

for what happened.

Sarah and I will

miss Mr. Friend,

when we are

riding our bikes.

Lots and Lots
and Lots of Love,
    Kari L. XOXOXO

"In our family an experience was not finished, not truly experienced, unless written down and shared with another."

—ANNE MORROW LINDBERGH

My friend had a miscarriage. I wonder what to send: e-mail, a card, flowers, a note, or to phone. I don't know how she feels.

She is probably grieving for a lost child, comforting other children, coping with medical complications, and unsure if she should "go public" with this very private sorrow. A card with a personal message written on it, or a short note offering sympathy without going into detail, will give her—and him—the chance to respond if they want to tell you more.

I received a lot of cards, notes, and letters from friends and relatives when my husband died. Do I have to answer each one with a note? Can't I just send out a printed card, or put a notice in the paper?

Yes, but a change in attitude may add pleasure to something that you are viewing right now as just one more chore. You don't *have to* answer with a note. You *get to* answer with a note. Death in the family is a disruptive implosion that damages your daily emotional resources; writing is a therapeutic activity that will help you heal. It helps you focus on a small, positive ritual through weeks of upheaval. In addition, remember that you are not the only person in pain; the people who wrote to you are also hurting inside, missing the person who died, anxious about you, and uncertain of what to do next to help. Your note, however brief, will connect you with them and with your late husband, so that the sum total of pain gets smaller. Writing helps everyone deal with loss. Even putting a printed acknowledgment into a hand-addressed envelope will make you feel a little better.

My dear Win,

I *loved* your letter and enjoyed walking back in time remembering the many good times we shared at the Alliance. We did some pretty outrageous things when the men would retire and we'd give them a send-off. Such class! Such style!

I'm busy with notes and getting some semblance of order to the house. Do you think I'll be smart enough to get the files in alphabetical order? Hmmm.

In a couple of weeks I'm having a supper party for all the musicians that provided such glorious music for Chuck's memorial service. I go to sleep at night hearing the music — such sweet comfort.

Take care, my lovely friend. N. ♡

My family and I are grateful for your gift of money in Chuck's honor and memory.

Chuck was loved and cherished by his family and friends,
admired and respected by many, and he will be greatly missed by all of us.

We have appreciated your caring concern through his illness
and have been uplifted with your love when it was time to say farewell.

God bless you and may His face shine upon you always.

Elizabeth and Jeff Malo
Lauren, Morgan and Nolan

John and Connie Buxton
Charles III

Trish and David De Biasse
Leigh, Drew, Nick and Drake

Cindy and Jim Henderson
Jessica and Jared

Sarah Buxton

My best friends are getting a divorce. I have a feeling they're going to each drop some of their former shared friends. Is writing going to do any good?

Send a short note to each of them. Express your best wishes for their new lives and say that you would like to stay in touch. Each of them may want to move on from some of the friends that remind them of their old life, but you've left the door open. Give them time. A note is neutral; it doesn't tempt them to draw you into a verbal recitation of their current battles the way a telephone call does, but leaves you available for the near future, when they both simmer down and get on with their lives.

I messed up so badly that I think I've permanently lost a friend.

You'd be surprised how a simple, personal handwritten apology can bring a friendship back from the brink of disaster. Don't overstate or understate your part in hurting them, but reaffirm that the friendship is important to you and you don't want to lose it. If they really want to break it off, at least you have let them know they matter to you. And they may want to think it over. But if you don't write at all, it's easy for them to assume that not only did you hurt them but you don't even know it or care. You don't need people out there feeling like that about you.

I ran over my neighbor's cat by accident. I want to apologize, but what if they sue me?

You can apologize in person if you think it would help. Sometimes, however, a note is better. But sleep on it, and check with your lawyer before you commit words to paper that could be used to prove more blame than you deserve. Keep a copy in case something you've written comes back to bite you. Sample wording: *I'm really sorry about Fluffy. I know how much she meant to you. I hope this won't spoil our friendship.*

Writing condolence letters and acknowledgments for condolence letters seems like an intolerable burden. Shouldn't people be excused from this extra chore at a time when their lives may already be disrupted?

It's what you must do when someone else needs it. Each time you write a condolence letter, it will get easier to do and clearer why it matters. Consider this: In November 1963 the newly widowed First Lady is reported to have written a note of condolence and gratitude to the widow of the police officer who was killed in arresting the president's assassin. If Jacqueline Kennedy could find the time to write to Mrs. Tippitt just a few days after organizing a state funeral and while comforting her own small children, can anyone else honestly claim to be too upset and busy to write?

"Why should it be such an effort to write to the people one loves I can't imagine. It's none at all to write to those who don't really count."

—KATHERINE MANSFIELD

Come Over

The completely handwritten invitation may be the only note that progress has replaced with something better. It is so easy to send (and reply to) e-mail invitations for personal affairs and printed invitations for formal parties that most people are not going to be offended by either one. And in addition, between these two extremes, there has emerged the supremely useful hybrid note, the *fill-in-the-blanks invitation*. Like an all-purpose Swiss Army knife of the social world, these preprinted forms are available in every stationery and card store, at every price level, for every conceivable specific or general kind of party; you can even design and print them out yourself. By writing with your own hand the information about what, where, when, who, and why, you create much of the same warmth as a handwritten note. Your recipient feels important and at the same time feels that the upcoming event is important too.

When you invite people to a party, whatever combination of print and handwriting you employ has to simultaneously carry two contradictory messages—that your readers are special individuals and that they are part of a group. Personal invitations almost always carry a combination of handwriting and printing, from the three hundred very formal engraved wedding invitations that are hand-addressed in italic calligraphy, through the hand-lettered notice with printed labels for your church potluck, to the twenty-five decorative cards you fill in by hand with details about your annual holiday cocktail party, right down to the three handwritten notes that confirm six phone calls arranging a small but elegant dinner party.

Wednesday, Sept 23

Dear Margaret,
      You hadn't said anything
about whirling dervishes! This
reception promises to be even
more exciting than my already
keen anticipation had
prepared me for. The caligraphy
sample is awesome.

      I am suggesting that
you and David come here
for a little supper beforehand –
about 6:30? Bob will scout
out a parking place near
Sakler – we can drive over for
what I'm sure will be a
fascinating evening.

                        Lyn

It's lovely of you to include us –

Be careful not to give the impression that the person is an insignificant member of a *large group* (unless of course that is the intent!). The clues that kill personal warmth include misspelled names, printed labels, machine addressing, the handwriting of a stranger, no handwriting inside or outside, machine imitation of handwritten script, second-class postage, flimsy paper, cheap printing. Business-size stationery and envelopes are not appropriate to social events. Metered postage and a window envelope are deadly. You create the friendliness of a *small group* if each invitation is at least partly handwritten, the address or the return address are handwritten, the paper is of good quality, the paper and ink are coordinated, and the wording is clear.

A hundred years ago, the sort of upper-class person who could afford to give formal parties usually had a social secretary who handled all the handwritten arrangements. Today, first-person "Please join us" has largely replaced third-person "Senator and Mrs. Holdforth Claghorn cordially request the honour of your presence." This archaic, formal, third-person wording still survives in the upper levels of government and the military, in upper-class England, and in conventional weddings.

The note you send as an invitation contains all kinds of signals about the party you're inviting the reader to, including signals that you may not even be consciously aware of. With even the simplest words, your choice of size, shape, and weight of paper, printing or handwriting or a combination of the two, numerals or words, even the addressing on the envelope, all hint at what to wear, who else is coming, and what will happen. Since anticipation is a big part of enjoyment, your invitation should give a visual preview of the event.

An invitation should tell the reader some essential facts about the party. However you choose to write it, it must contain the location, the date, and the time; what the event is about; the dress code; who is really giving the party; to whom to respond; who is included in the invitation (whose names are on the envelope). An invitation also carries a lot of implied information about the other people being invited, much of it the kind of thing a polite person is not supposed to ask out loud: What kind of people will be there, whom can I bring with me, how many other people are receiving this invitation, is a gift expected, am I being invited or just notified, will I be missed if I don't show up, do they really want me, how formal is it, how much is being spent and by whom, how exclusive is the guest list.

You almost can't send an invitation too early! (Most people worry about sending them too late.) In general, the larger or more formal the affair, the earlier the invitation should arrive: three weeks for a small sitdown dinner or a big standup party, six weeks for a wedding, coming-of-age, or anniversary. But as a rule of thumb, if you want to invite people to an event more than six weeks before it is going to happen so that they can make travel arrangements or participate in planning the event, then send a "hold the date" postcard or e-mail. Give the date and the event and your name or group. If you keep it very brief, they will get the message that a more complete invitation will follow. Make sure your return address is clear, because an additional virtue of the "hold the date" mailing is that it not only helps people hold the date but also lets you get the bugs out of the addresses on your mailing list before the really important invitations are mailed.

PHRASES TO INCLUDE IN INVITATION NOTES

Do Say:

Please join us

We would be pleased

You are invited, cordially invited

It's a celebration

Request the pleasure of your company

Celebrate with us

Invite you, joyfully invite you, warmly invite you

Don't Say:

The honour of your presence [except for the most formal wedding]

No gifts; send money

Would you join us [because then you should put a question mark at the end]

It is tempting to tinker with conventional invitation wording, to try to modernize it or give it your own creative tone. But the risk is generally not worth the reward—it's too easy to bog down in swamps of awkward phrasing and unintended clunkers. Read

it out loud, or have someone else read it to you, before you write
it by hand.

⁂

*My handwriting is really messy. Should I hire someone to address my
daughter's wedding invitations?*

Use hired handwriting the way you would use a rented function room or a professional caterer; of course your own touch is
always nicer but it just may not be possible. A calligrapher can design the original artwork for a printed invitation or fill in a printed
form, and address the mailing envelopes. Also, a family member
or close friend can volunteer to help address envelopes.

Please

A special kind of handwritten note asks the reader to
do something for the writer. It is sometimes the hardest note to realize that you should write but the easiest
to phrase, especially since many times you will be writing to ask
on behalf of someone else. It may be particularly effective because it does not put pressure on the person to decide immediately to do what you ask. And generally people are happy to do
the thing you are asking, but often would not do it themselves
without being prompted by a handwritten note.

There are three main categories of please notes:

I need. *Request for a recommendation or something else
that will benefit the writer.*

He/she needs. *A letter of introduction that asks the reader to do something that will benefit another person.*

They/we need. *Fund-raiser, please contribute money to my organization. Call for volunteers; please do some work for my organization.*

Q&A

I need a letter of recommendation. I can call my professor or just ask her in person. Why do I have to write a note?
Because when people write a letter of recommendation, they first get out everything they have in your file to refresh their memory of your pluses and minuses. Your request, in your personal handwriting, will be on top of the plus pile. In your note you might also include reminders about what you would like the person to emphasize about you; this makes their task easier.

Beyond please: the *help!* note. If you've got to get help pronto, don't worry about what you write on or how you word it. Desperate materials may help you to emphasize your dire distress. John F. Kennedy wrote on a coconut husk to ask for rescue when his crew from PT 109 was marooned on an island in the Pacific during World War II.

"Writing is but a different name for conversation."

—LAURENCE STERNE, *TRISTRAM SHANDY* (1760)

I want to say more than please, I want to say pretty please with cream and sugar on it. Can I send flowers, candy, or some other gift with my please note?

Please notes are almost always classier and more effective on their own—you're asking for something on the strength of your relationship with the reader, something you would be glad to do in return if the situation were reversed. A bouquet subtracts sincerity from a please note; a bouquet adds sincerity to a thank-you note.

Only very young children can legitimately write a note that asks for free things for themselves. Most of these notes will take the form of birthday lists sent to near relatives and Christmas lists sent to Santa Claus.

If you are writing to ask someone older, richer, or more famous than you for something, please read page 127 to learn how to write a fan note.

To say please, use your best stationery and keep your handwriting small and neat. Phrase your please note so that it is clear what you want and easy for the reader to say yes. Don't get all tangled up in euphemisms, formal courtesies, and apologies for asking. If you have trouble asking for things for yourself, write a rough draft first as if you were asking on behalf of someone else.

Dear Mom + Dad,
    I <u>Really</u> hate it here at Camp. I miss you all. the food is terrible, the counsellors despise me and there are to many bugs. Come get me Right away!
      Love
      Abby

PHRASES TO INCLUDE IN
YOUR REQUEST FOR HELP

Do Say:

I would be grateful for

Can you help me with

May I request

Would it be convenient

On behalf of my group

Let me know if this is inconvenient

It would be very kind of you to

Please allow my child to be absent from school

Please let me know if I should redirect my request

Would you be willing

Don't Say:

Dear Occupant

Here's a list of my demands

Why don't you just

I want you to

I need this right away

I don't have time to read your book for my term paper next week, so . . .

Please send me an expensive object with your autograph on it

You have to

You'd better

You don't know me but

I need you to

Can you rush this

And while you're at it

I Love You, I Love You Not, I Like You

Handwritten *love letters* used to be the main outlet for those lucky couples who had found each other but were not married yet, for spouses separated by distance, and for those whose love could not lead to matrimony. Before people met online and courted through e-mail, and before they could whisper on the telephone, couples wrote each other dozens, hundreds, sometimes thousands of personal, affectionate, ecstatic notes. Some even started their courtship with an opening letter to introduce themselves and met the object of their affections only after getting to know each other on paper. Twenty-first-century e-mail mirrors that nineteenth-century way of getting acquainted, with some of the same social safeguards built in. But e-mailed sentiments, however private and timely, can't convey the sense of who is writing, the immediacy and intimacy and intensity, that you can create by mailing those same words in your handwriting. And you may find that pen and paper inspire you to write better words than the keyboard.

> May 1, 00
>
> Dearest Michael,
>   The bouquet on the doorstep is
> the nicest thing anybody has
> done for me in weeks. I am
> so glad you live on my planet,
> and that we found each other,
> and that we fell in love. And
> that we both like daisies.
>   Yours
>   Maureen

A handwritten love note is a keepsake; with a few extra minutes you can shine a light on your relationship and capture the moment forever. A handwritten love note is an opportunity; you can look for occasions to use it instead of, or in addition to, your other ways of being together. A handwritten love note is an adventure; if you start by simply writing down what you usually say, you may find yourself discovering words to write down that you wouldn't have thought of saying out loud.

In addition, a handwritten note is statistically America's favorite way to say "I love you." In a survey of a thousand adults, nearly half preferred a handwritten note, compared to 40 percent who liked their Valentine's Day sentiments to arrive on greeting cards. E-mail cards and e-mail messages were a distant third and fourth place at 9 percent and 2 percent.

And a handwritten love note is versatile; anyone can send love on paper. Parents who pack lunch boxes, couples who e-mail each other from adjoining rooms, siblings who trade insults as an art form, and kids who spend their first week away from home, all can enjoy putting some of the underlying love on paper.

A handwritten note is appropriate anytime, from the start of a relationship right through wedding day and beyond. Stay particularly alert to the way a handwritten note can focus the blur of daily interaction to mark some special moment like a minor anniversary or a shared achievement.

Once in a while, try handwriting the same things you'd say online to your girlfriend or boyfriend. If nothing else, it will get their attention; if you've got competition, it's probably safe to say

In the course of an eighteen-month infatuation, early twentieth-century novelist Edith Wharton and her lover exchanged over three thousand handwritten notes. In an era when city mail was delivered six times a day, lovers and ordinary people could communicate with notes in almost real time.

that not many of the others are sending handwritten notes to the one you love. Plus, hardly anyone saves sweet little e-mails with a red ribbon around them.

Dear John. It's Over

When it is time to break off a love affair, sending a handwritten breakup note may seem like an oxymoron, using a medium that says "I care enough about you to communicate in the nicest way" to send the actual words that say "I don't care enough about you to even want to communicate with you any longer." But if you like to do things in a humane and classy way no matter whom you are dealing with, the best way to say it's over may be in your own handwriting. And learning to be civilized, even when the person you are dealing with hasn't been, lets you reassure yourself that he is the one, not you, who has lost something valuable by acting badly.

Of course, none of your parting words should go down on paper if they could be shown around, fall into the wrong hands, or be used against you in court. Be honest but restrained. Remember, you are entitled to kill the relationship, not the person. Go ahead and scribble that blistering, apoplectic, needy, and self-incriminating note—and put it into a drawer. Then write a second civilized, impersonal, mildly regretful note, in handwriting that doesn't look agitated, on civilized stationery, and mail that one.

Be clear in your head before you write. Now is the time to ask honestly for anything that you think will repair the connection you once had, or say without ambiguity why you think it should be ended. If you want to put your own positive spin on things, this may be your last chance. You'll be glad in the future that you took the high road.

WORDING TO ANCHOR YOUR BREAKUP NOTES

Do Say:

It didn't work out

After a lot of thought

I'm sorry we're not really meant for each other

We're not headed anywhere

I don't love you anymore

It's been good but it's over

Your socks are on your windshield to remind you that the rest of your stuff is packed in the car.

I wish things had turned out differently

This really isn't working for me because

I am feeling hurt because

It's too bad that it didn't turn out differently

Could have, would have, should have

Don't Say:

I hate you

I never loved you

Why are you doing this to me

I'm going to kill myself

I, me, mine

@#%&

Yours, Love, Devotedly, etc.

Q & A

 I love this guy; we go everywhere together and get along great. My only problem is he smokes a lot. Is is rude to ask him to quit with a note?

Lots of things you can't bring up with someone you see every day might get their attention if written in a note. Choose your words with care to avoid writing a complaint note, but be warm and firm.

Isn't it kind of cowardly to break up with a note?

Not if it lets you get your feelings down on paper in a form the other person can understand. At some point in the past you were in love with them. Now you're not. Let them save face; leave them some dignity. Even if you don't owe it to them, you owe it to yourself to say good-bye with class.

I'm kind of shy. Should I write this girl a note to ask her out?

You can keep your note casual and specific, simply asking her out for a concert, dinner, or event on a particular day. Respectful shyness is not the worst personality trait to reveal to a prospective date. Don't feel you have to declare your interest or make statements you might feel funny about if she shared them with someone else. Be careful of overstating your feelings on paper before you get to know someone. But as soon as you are acquainted, a note is an elegant, considerate way to invite her out. It gives the occasion extra importance without putting pressure on her, and if you continue to go out, it gives the two of you an extra channel of communication for the future.

The World War II espionage team in *The Man Who Never Was* added a carefully crafted love note from a fictional girlfriend to the personal possessions of a fabricated spy, and then carefully "aged" it to give it the convincing patina that it would have acquired from being carried with him everywhere. The whole persona they created helped fool the Nazis into preparing for the D day invasion at a landing far from Normandy.

I Like You

To express affection rather than love, you can tone down the love note into the *like note*. Sometimes a note can simply reaffirm a friendship or recognize a relationship that you enjoy. If you would buy a preprinted friendship card for a friend, why not write similar words in your own handwriting? Friendship notes can keep a long distance friendship alive between people who see each other only once in a while, or even create a friendship between pen pals in other countries.

You Don't Know Me but I Like You

There's even an art to writing a *fan letter* to a celebrity, a one-time note in a one-way relationship. Your note can go to the soap opera actress who needs a full-time assistant just to organize and acknowledge the thousands of fan letters that her character receives, or to the retired high school literature teacher who may not realize what a difference he made in your career. Try to picture the person who will be opening your note before you fire off that note into the blue. What are you really trying to accomplish? Do you just want to send admiration or do you want something specific?

Your fan note will bridge some distance; try to judge how likely it is that the person even knows who you are. Different wording is appropriate for various relationships: a fan to a movie star, a reader to an author, a spectator to a performer, a student to a former teacher. Neat handwriting, plain paper, conventional phrasing, correct spelling, and accurate addressing will help you avoid giving the impression of crank mail. Don't gush or presume. Be brief, be specific, ask clearly for what you may want but don't ask for much, don't get personal, don't ask for favors. Make it easy to reply but be aware that they may not respond. A very busy person may handwrite a reply in the margins of your note and send it back to you, or delegate the response to a staffer, without intending to be rude.

A fan note is fun to write, whether you ever hear back. Don't expect to strike up a friendship. A famous person usually has enough friends; no famous person ever has enough fans. Your note, if considerate and respectful, will be welcome even to the biggest celebrity.

BASIC PHRASES TO ANCHOR YOUR FAN LETTER

Do Say:

I like your work

I enjoyed your most recent [book, recording, performance, show]

I particularly like [specific thing] in your work

I learned a lot in your physics course in 1996

If you are ever in my town, please let me take you to lunch [not likely]

I have every one of your books

Your work made a big difference to me

Do you have a photograph you could autograph for me

Could I send you my portfolio/proposal/recording

May I write to you with a specific proposal about some future project

Would you put me on your mailing list

Don't Say:

I have this personal feeling about you and me

I've been following you

I bought your book for a dollar from a store that sells rejects

I checked your book out from the library

I had a dream about you

I haven't read your book

Would you look at my portfolio, read my manuscript, play my tape (I have enclosed it in this envelope)

I, me, mine

Please autograph some expensive object and send it to me

Please give my brother-in-law a job in your band

Margaret Mitchell, author of *Gone with the Wind*, never wrote a second book partly because she spent her time answering every fan letter she received.

Albert Einstein wasn't just smart; he was a genius. He usually answered handwritten inquiries by return of post (i.e., the next day).

Q&A

 I want to write to someone I met in an Internet chat room. I think seeing our handwriting would tell us a lot about each other.

Don't get into a handwritten correspondence using your home address with anyone you have met only on the Internet. Though you may believe handwriting offers a valuable insight into anyone's character, the risk of having an unknown person know where you live is not worth it.

I wrote a note after our second date and never heard back. What do I do now?

You could write again, but maybe this lack of a note is equal to a virtual Dear John; the person didn't warm to you and doesn't want to pursue it and is letting you know about it in the simplest way.

If you wrote a note that should have gotten a response and didn't, wait a reasonable interval of time and try a different medium. In a casual encounter, a telephone call, or e-mail about another subject, mention that you wondered what they would answer to your note. But be low-key. Remarkably few notes go astray nowadays, but they do sometimes take extra days to arrive and more days for the reader to get organized to write back.

If you find yourself in a dramatic, intriguing, or life-threatening situation because you can't tell if your love note got delivered, you may actually be a character in a story. Literature is full of lovelorn people who lose their chance for happiness because they don't realize their love note has gone astray. The mother in *The Beauty Queen of Leenane* who steals the note left by a suitor for her daughter; the narrator in *Green Dolphin Street* who in a drunken haze writes a proposal of marriage to the wrong sister; Celie in *The Color Purple*, whose husband has hidden every letter from her beloved sister. Undelivered notes generally don't cause such drama, except, of course, for the fuss when you "forget" to write a thank-you note to your grandmother for those socks.

I'm worried about my note falling into the wrong hands.

Then use e-mail if you have individual access. Or deliver the note by hand. But your loved one can still break trust and show it around if things go wrong. So keep your writing R-rated; be discreet and coherent even in private correspondence.

In generations past, when a love affair or an engagement was broken off, the civilized thing to do was to return the writer all letters that they had sent.

I've been Dear Johned. How do I respond to a breakup note?

Sometimes you can tell whether there's any chance of rescuing the relationship. Look for phrases that keep the door open like "It is too bad that it didn't turn out differently" or "could have," "would have," "should have." A short, simply worded, neatly handwritten apology, accompanied by a little bouquet of flowers, might delay your execution.

Congratulations

An informal variation on the personal notes that say "I love you" and "I like you" is the note that says specifically *I like what you did*. Don't be content with just saying "good job" out loud; it is important to get congratulations and approval down in writing, where the person can enjoy them over and over, and show them to others. You can express every level of formality from the most casual *Wow!* of a close friend's note, through the *from all of us* greeting card signed by everyone in the office, through the *good job* letter that goes into an em-

> Dear Jeannie, May 28, 01
>
> You did an absolutely great job on the talk. I hope you heard back from some of the people who went home with lists in their hands and smiles on their faces.
>
> I'm looking forward to your next triumph.
>
> Sincerely,
> Margaret

ployee file, to the *Whereas . . . now therefore* retirement scroll that celebrates the achievements of a lifetime in gold leaf and authentic parchment.

Congratulations are particularly nice to put on paper when people have their first child. The parents, if they keep their wits about them, can put a few such notes away in a memory box for the child to read later—a guaranteed treasure to make any growing child feel important and connected.

The opposite of the congratulations note that says I like what you did is the criticism note that says I don't like what you did. Resist the cowardly urge to send complaints in a note. Unless you know the person very, very well, you may come to regret putting negative suggestions, even mild ones, into writing. Furthermore, the negativity of the sentiments will actually worsen your handwriting. The solitariness of writing makes it seem that the person is not responding; this may betray you into saying more than you need to say, more than you feel, and more than the reader is prepared to accept. The Arabic saying goes, "Carve praise in marble, trace criticism in the dust." Display your congratulations on paper in writing but confide your criticisms privately in person. If you feel you just have to put bad news or criticism into a note, mix it with praise or good news and *put the good news first*.

Don't fill your notes with complaints about your own health; you can't be sure that the reader attaches the same importance to them that you do. Do not write complaints about a third person; some mail gets read by others. And most of all, don't complain in a note about not receiving a reply to a previous note. People have their own reasons for not writing back. Although you may yearn to hear from someone, the "why haven't you written" note usually doesn't work.

"Behold me going to write you as handsome a letter as I can. Wish me luck."

—JANE AUSTEN TO

FRANCIS AUSTEN, 1813

VI

Thinking of You:

Beyond the Note

If you like expressing yourself with a handwritten note, you will love exploring what other forms it can take and what else it can help you to say on paper. You can stretch or shrink the handwritten note beyond its basic format to capture a wide range of feelings, deliver a variety of information, and strengthen many kinds of relationships. Your handwritten words can say "thinking of you" in many creative ways.

Notes in Costumes

Notes don't always have to stick to the middle ground of traditional materials and conventional phrasing. They can run the gamut of formality from *guess what!* to *it gives me great pleasure to inform you,* and range in size from several words to several pages. You can experiment with unusual stationery, write on huge sheets or tiny notepaper, use white ink on dark paper, start round-robin group letters for family news, send whole sheets flat in large envelopes, or even present a beautifully lettered parchment page of compliments rolled up and tied with red ribbon. Perfumed ink adds glamour, and sealing wax makes a note look official.

Supernotes

Sometimes your words overflow the limits of the note and fill several pages of an old-fashioned handwritten letter with writing that is not prompted by a specific occasion but that simply tells about topics of mutual interest to writer and reader. This kind of personal, full-length, more-than-a-note is especially welcome to a young person away from home the first time or far from home, to an older person, to someone at an important milestone in life, and to someone who means a lot to you. A real letter is often the best way to maintain the long-term commitment and enduring warmth that characterize the close friendships of compatible people who live apart. You can gracefully mix daily details with overarching themes. Your handwriting makes you vividly present to your reader, who becomes almost a part of your inner voice if you write letters regularly as an extension of journal writing. In addition, your handwriting improves with the practice, security, and happy thoughts.

If you like to write letters, or would like to try, take precautions to make it physically easy to write at length. Set yourself up with plenty of big, smooth, plain, good-quality stationery sheets, optional guidelines to lay under the sheets, a fountain pen, a list of topics. Help yourself make time for writing by incorporating rituals into your schedule: an annual date to catch up or the custom of a birthday update, an agreed-upon interval for checking in with each other; a weekly rereading of your calendar for what you did that you'd like to think about and share. If you are already keeping a journal, it's a natural next step to take some of those thoughts you have put into words for yourself and rephrase them for others.

Or perhaps letter writing to others will inspire you to start keeping a journal for yourself. Many writers got started by focusing their thoughts on one person. Anne Frank, for instance, began writing her diary as letters to a fictional friend, Kitty, while she found a writing style that ultimately would let her address her thoughts to herself and to succeeding generations of readers.

Sometimes a handwritten letter is the very best way to carry a message from one person to many people. The *open letter* offers the personal touch of the writer's own handwriting while it uses the wording that makes a personal experience public; it is meant to be circulated or displayed or reproduced, to reach a number of readers.

Some people write to each other for the sheer joy of using pen and paper. Authors, poets, and writers have always used words on paper more readily than the average person and often relish sending handwritten notes and letters as an extension of their daily creative dance with the written word. A particular interest in how the writing itself looks on the page can be seen in the notes that calligraphers, composers, and typographers send to each other. Visual artists of all kinds choose interesting paper, letterheads, and ink when they write, pay special attention to it when they read, and add drawings freely to their text. Pen col-

PARTIAL TRANSCRIPT OF LETTER FROM
PRESIDENT RONALD REAGAN
TO THE AMERICAN PEOPLE

Nov. 5, 1994

My Fellow Americans,

I have recently been told that I am one of the millions of Americans who will be afflicted with Alzheimer's Disease.

Upon learning this news, Nancy & I had to decide whether as private citizens we would keep this a private matter or whether we would make this news known in a public way.

In the past Nancy suffered from breast cancer and I had my cancer surgeries. We found through our open disclosures we were able to raise public awareness. We were happy that as a result many more people underwent testing. They were treated in early stages and able to return to normal, healthy lives.

So now, we feel it is important to share it with you. In opening our hearts, we hope this might promote greater awareness of this condition. Perhaps it will encourage a clearer understanding of the individuals and families who are affected by it.

At the moment I feel just fine. I intend to live the remainder of the years God gives me on this earth doing the things I have always done. I will continue to share life's journey with my beloved Nancy and my family. I plan to enjoy the great outdoors and stay in touch with my friends and supporters.

RONALD REAGAN

Nov. 5, 1994

My Fellow Americans,

I have recently been told that I am one of the millions of Americans who will be afflicted with Alzheimer's Disease.

Upon learning this news, Nancy & I had to decide whether as private citizens we would keep this a private matter or whether we would make this news known in a public way.

In the past Nancy suffered from breast cancer and I had my cancer surgeries. We found through our open disclosures we were able to raise public awareness. We were happy that as a result many more people underwent testing. They were treated in early stages and able to return to normal, healthy lives.

So now, we feel it is important to share it with you. In opening our hearts, we hope this might promote greater awareness of this condition. Perhaps it will encourage a clearer understanding of the individuals and families who are affected by it.

At the moment I feel just fine. I intend to live the remainder of the years God gives me on this earth doing the things I have always done. I will continue to share life's journey with my beloved Nancy and my family. I plan to enjoy the great outdoors and stay in touch with my friends and supporters.

lectors and stamp collectors may elevate the envelope itself into an art form.

Children and teenagers share note-writing protocols all their own. They experiment with materials, script, wording. They try fresh new salutations, acronyms, emotions, and codes. Examples: *Hi Dude, Hello, LOL, SWAK,* :), :(, *evol.* Young writers appropriately find every excuse to experiment with the medium, try out different identities, rebel, create, stay connected with one another. They push the envelope to reinvent the handwritten note for the next generation.

Note writers may also share a private language and graphic style within their own family, relaxing the usual rules to incorporate handwritten notes into the margins of duplicated family news and other people's letters. Family notes can also be delivered in ritualistic ways, in recycled envelopes, on the fridge, in a teapot, or on the steering wheel.

A family letter that occupies a niche all its own is the annual holiday letter that tells relatives, friends, coworkers, and sometimes virtual strangers what activities a family has accomplished during the year. These letters are as distinctively American as fruitcake, and, like fruitcake, have their fans and their critics.

Fictional characters write to each other with an inspiring variety of thinking-of-you notes too. You can eavesdrop on their correspondence in books, plays, and movies like *Griffin and Sabine, The Jolly Postman, 84 Charing Cross Road, The Color Purple, The Documents in the Case, Love Letters by A. R. Gurney, The Screwtape Letters.*

While you enjoy the script you see in fictional notes, don't underestimate the inspiration you can find by reading typeset transcriptions of the phrasing of real notes. Pay attention to what a handwritten note, in the hands of a master wordsmith speaking through ordinary fictional characters, can express. You can also seek out the collected and selected letters of many great figures of the past, to enjoy their personalities through their words. Most of these books include an illustration of a sample of the person's handwriting. And many libraries and museums will let you visit their archives to see the real letters of famous people.

Semi-notes

The note can get smaller without entirely losing its strength. The *postcard* also has a small, unique role to help you to stay in touch. Most postcards, of course, are open to the casual reader. Your tone will be breezy and your writing may need to be compressed. (You can make your postcards seem more important and more private by just enclosing them in an envelope. And then you can actually say something personal in the extra space.)

The decision to take your address list along on vacation with you on preprinted labels to speed up your postcard writing should be based on what message you think your friends will read into it. How do you feel when a postcard comes in your mail addressed with a label? Does it say that the writer wanted to relax and make postcard writing as streamlined as possible, or does it say that even on vacation the writer was too busy to write three extra lines of script (and wanted you to know it)? You can decide for yourself.

Pay attention to the bulletin board in your office to see if a postcard from you to your coworkers is expected from you on holiday. If it feels like an obligation, your wording can turn it into an opportunity. It can be a lively and constructive part of your ongoing connections with each other, including a variety of buzzwords, in jokes, current preoccupations, and remembered interests.

An even shorter version of the thinking-of-you note is the expanded to-and-from note that adds a brief greeting or explanation to a gift-wrapped object: flowers, wine, candy. The note in-

Dear Margaret,

Congratulations! A very interesting, well-planned and successful presentation.

Much love,
Margaret

Maybe you saw the enclosed in the Yale Alumni Magazine?

tensifies the personal significance of the gesture and may be kept long after the gift is used up. You can also use from-the-desk-of notes attached to clippings and written material that you collect and then pass on with your comments, or reach for the shortest version of the handwritten note, the sticky note. All of these mininotes, micronotes, and nanonotes can be crafted with the same care as a full-size note and can add a touch of your hand to whatever they accompany.

Still Thinking of You: Writing to the People Who Can't Write Back

The art of the handwritten note can connect you to the people in your life in a hundred heartwarming ways. You can strengthen relationships, clarify your own thoughts, or mark important milestones.

Like any art, writing by hand feels as good to do it as to view it. Writing a note does so much good for you yourself that you can even benefit from writing the kind of note that can't be mailed, addressed to people who exist only in your memory or your imagination.

If you have found that pen and paper help you say words you might not otherwise express, you can rise above the routines of daily life by writing to yourself, to a child not born yet, to someone who has died, to Santa, and to God. Writing is the best way to put into words what is in your mind and your heart.

"Letters mingle souls."

—JOHN DONNE

"Let us all then leave behind letters of love and friendship, family and devotion, hope and consolation, so that future generations will know what we valued and believed and achieved."

—MARIAN WRIGHT EDELMAN,
FROM THE FOREWORD OF
LETTERS OF A NATION

At a time when our country mourned our great losses and looked to gather strength for the days ahead, we saw many images of handwritten notes—thank yous to rescue workers, goodbyes to loved ones and pleas for hope and courage. The power of these heartfelt expressions, written by hand, is clear. They serve as evidence of our collective humanity and offer some solace to our wounded souls. M.S., September 2001

Associated Press, AP

BIBLIOGRAPHY

Ahlberg, Jane. *The Jolly Postman*. Boston: Little, Brown, 1987.

Bantock, Nick. *Griffin and Sabine, An Extraordinary Correspondence*. San Francisco: Chronicle Books, 1991.

Clark, Beverly. *Heartfelt Thank Yous: Perfect Ways for Brides to Say Thank You*. Emeryville, CA: Wilshire Publications, 2001.

Cobb, Nancy. *The Reader's Digest Letter Writer Starter Set*. Pleasant-ville, NY: Reader's Digest Children's Books, 1994.

Dolnick, Barrie, and Donald Baack. *How to Write a Love Letter: Putting What's in Your Heart on Paper*. New York: Harmony Books, 2001.

Donelley, Nina Hartman. *I Never Know What to Say*. New York: Ballantine, 1987.

Geordie, Tom. *Italic Handwriting*. London: Studio Vista, 1955.

Getty, Barbara, and Inga Dubay. *Basic Italic*. Italic Handwriting Series. Portland, OR: Portland State University, 1980.

Goffman, Irving. *The Presentation of Self in Everyday Life*. Anchor, 1959.

Harding, Rachel, and Mary Dyson, eds. *A Book of Condolences; Classic Letters of Bereavement*. New York: Continuum Publishing, 1981.

Keillor, Garrison. "How to write a letter," from *We Are Still Married*. New York: Viking Penguin, 1982.

Kubler-Ross, Elisabeth. *On Death and Dying*. New York: Macmillan, 1969.

Let's Learn to Write Script. A Wipe-it-off Practice Book. Troll Associates.

Lewis, C. S. *A Grief Observed*. New York: HarperCollins, 2000.

Maggio, Rosalie. *Great Letters for Every Occasion*. New York: Prentice Hall Press, 1999.

Morris, Edmund, "This Living Hand." *The New Yorker*, January 16, 1995.

Piljac, Pamela A. *Bride's Thank You Guide: Thank You Writing Made Easy.* Chicago: Chicago Review Press, 1993.

Standage, Tom. *The Victorian Internet.* Berkley Books, 1998.

Strunk, William, and E. B. White. *The Elements of Style.* New York: Macmillan, 1957.

Taylor, Judy, ed. *Letters to Children from Beatrix Potter.* London: Penguin, 1992.

Thornton, Tamara Plakins. *Handwriting in America, A Cultural History.* New Haven: Yale University Press, 1996.

MARGARET SHEPHERD is a noted calligrapher and author with an impressive roster of high-profile clients. She has published fourteen instruction books for calligraphers of all levels. Her previous books, including the best-selling *Learning Calligraphy*, are done in hand-lettered text. She has researched, taught, written, and freelanced extensively, and has exhibited her work in many museums and galleries. She lives in Boston.